A-Z LINCOLN

CONTENTS

Key to Map Pages	2-3
Map Pages	4-37
Large Scale City Centre	38
Index	
Villag...	56
& sel...	

REFERENCE

A Road	A57	Car Park (Selected)	P
Proposed		Church or Chapel	†
B Road	B1188	Cycleway (Selected)	
Dual Carriageway		Fire Station	■
One-way Street		Hospital	H
Traffic flow on A roads is also indicated by a heavy line on the driver's left.		House Numbers (A & B Roads only)	2 75
Restricted Access		Information Centre	i
Pedestrianized Road		National Grid Reference	490
Track & Footpath		Police Station	▲
Residential Walkway		Post Office	★
Railway	Station / Level Crossing	Toilet: without facilities for the Disabled / with facilities for the Disabled	▽ / ▽
Built-Up Area		Educational Establishment	
Local Authority Boundary		Hospital or Hospice	
Posttown Boundary		Industrial Building	
Postcode Boundary (within Posttown)		Leisure or Recreational Facility	
		Place of Interest	
Map Continuation	12 Large Scale City Centre 38	Public Building	
		Shopping Centre or Market	
		Other Selected Buildings	

SCALE

Map Pages 4-37 1:19,000	Map Page 38 1:9,500
0 ¼ ½ Mile	0 ⅛ ¼ Mile
0 250 500 750 Metres	0 100 200 300 Metres
3.33 inches (8.47cm) to 1 mile 5.26cm to 1km	6.67 inches (16.94cm) to 1 mile 10.53 cm to 1km

Copyright of Geographers' A-Z Map Company Limited

Fairfield Road, Borough Green, Sevenoaks, Kent TN15 8PP
Telephone: 01732 781000 (Enquiries & Trade Sales)
             01732 783422 (Retail Sales)
www.a-zmaps.co.uk

Ordnance Survey® This product includes mapping data licensed from Ordnance Survey® with the permission of the Controller of Her Majesty's Stationery Office.

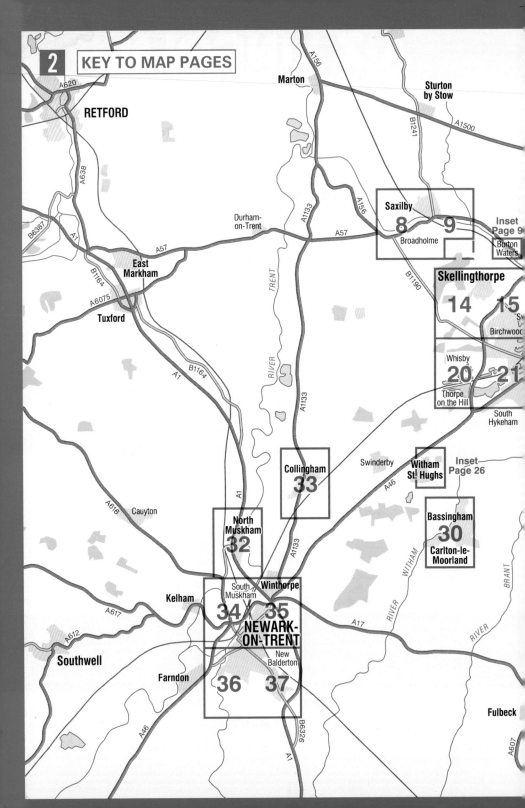

2 **KEY TO MAP PAGES**

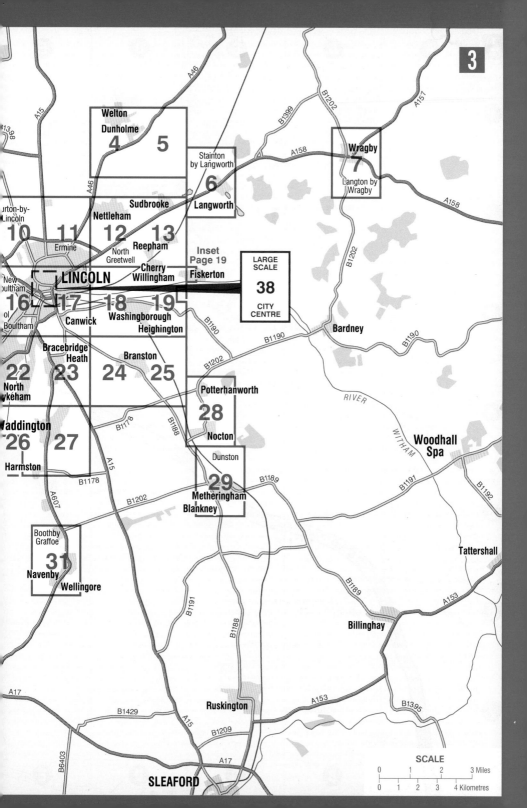

3

Welton
Dunholme
4 **5**

Stainton
by Langworth
6

Wragby
7

Langton by
Wragby

A158

Sudbrooke
Langworth
Nettleham
urton-by-Lincoln
10 **11** **12** **13**
Ermine
Reepham
North Greetwell
Inset
Page 19

LARGE
SCALE
38
CITY
CENTRE

New oultham
LINCOLN
Cherry Willingham
Fiskerton

16 **17** **18** **19**
Canwick
Washingborough
Heighington
Boultham

Bardney

Bracebridge
Heath
Branston
22 **23** **24** **25**
North ykeham

RIVER

Potterhanworth
28
Nocton
WITHAM
Woodhall
Spa

addington
26 **27**
Harmston
Dunston
29
Metheringham
Blankney
Tattershall

Boothby
Graffoe
31
Navenby
Wellingore
Billinghay

Ruskington

A153

SLEAFORD

SCALE
0   1   2   3 Miles
0   1   2   3   4 Kilometres

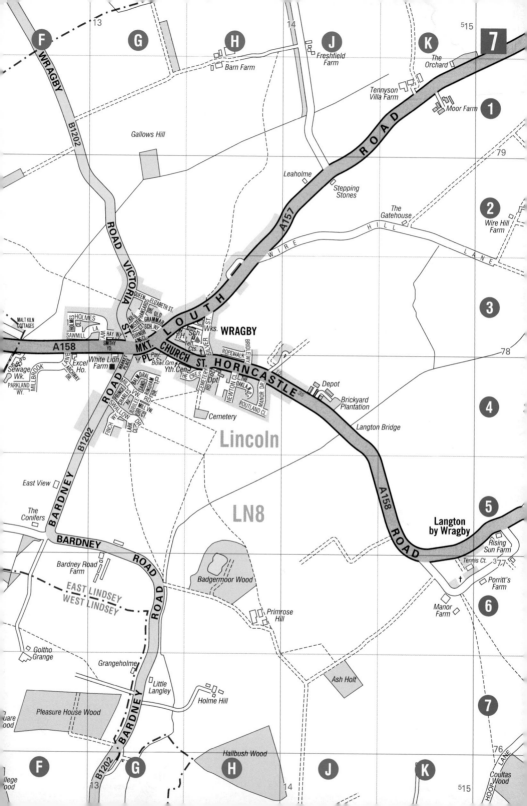

7

WRAGBY

The Orchard

Moor Farm

Tennyson Villa Farm

Freshfield Farm

Barn Farm

Gallows Hill

WRAGBY ROAD

B1202

A157

Leaholme

Stepping Stones

The Gatehouse

Wire Hill Farm

WIRE HILL LANE

VICTORIA ST

ROAD

MALT KILN COTTAGES

HOLMES CL

HOLMES RD

SAWMILL LA

HAY WY

QUEEN ELIZABETH ST

KNIGHT MASKELL ST

DIX RD

THE OLD GRAMMAR SCH LA

TURNOR CL

SILVER ST

Inf Sch

WKS

Prim Sch

Cts

Pav

Bowl. Grn

Yth. Cen.

ROPEWALK

BRIDLE WY

A158

SMITHY YD

PL

CHURCH ST

MKT

ST LOUTH

Pay

HORNCASTLE

Excel Ho.

White Lion Farm

ARCHWAY DR

MILLBROOK

SEWAGE WK.

PARKLAND WY.

BALMORAL CL

DE VERDUN AVE

JUBILEE CL

CHARLES CL

DRAYTON RD

ALMOND CL

NEWTON CL

THE CRES

MANOR DR

OAKLEA

DEPT

CONISTON RD

RUTLAND CL

MILL VW

MILL CL

FINCH CL

SWALLOW

WILLOW LA

LARK CL

Cemetery

Depot

Brickyard Plantation

Langton Bridge

A158 ROAD

Langton by Wragby

Rising Sun Farm

Tennis Ct.

Porritt's Farm

Manor Farm

Lincoln

LN8

East View

The Conifers

BARDNEY ROAD

B1202

BARDNEY ROAD

Bardney Road Farm

EAST LINDSEY

WEST LINDSEY

Badgermoor Wood

Goltho Grange

Grangeholme

Little Langley

Holme Hill

Primrose Hill

Ash Holt

Pleasure House Wood

...quare ...ood

...llege ...ood

Halibush Wood

Coultas Wood

HOOP LANE

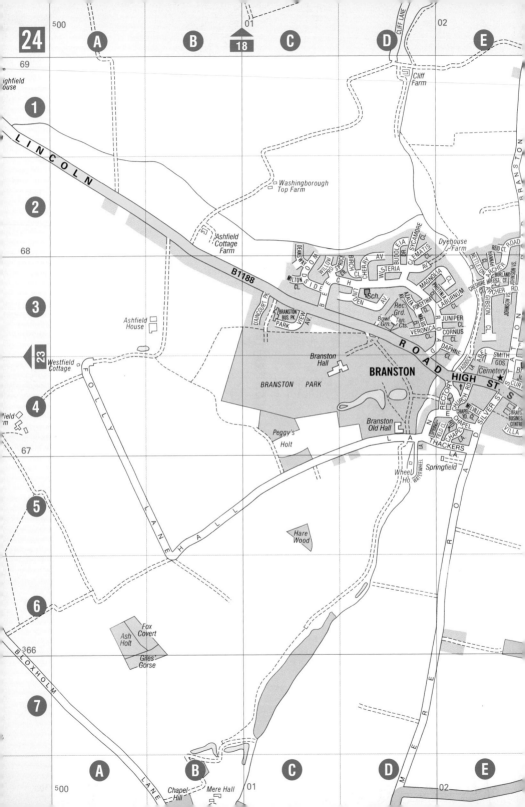

24

A **B** **C** **D** **E**

500   01   02

69

18

ighfield ouse

1

LINCOLN

2

68

Washingborough Top Farm

B1188

Ashfield Cottage Farm

Cliff Farm

Dyehouse Farm

REID CT.

3

Ashfield House

Sch

Rec. Grd.

Bowl. Grn.

Ten. Cts.

BRANSTON BUS. PK.

DAINCOURT PK.

MILTON CL.

DEANS WAY

BEECH

WILLOW

SPRUCE

BIRCH

LARCH

OZIER

ALDER

CHERRY

WISTERIA

BUDDLEIA DR.

CLEMATIS

SYCAMORE AV.

MAGNOLIA

PHOTINIA

FORSYTHIA

LABURNUM CL.

JUNIPER CL.

VERONICA

CORNUS CL.

DAPHNE CL.

NETTLEHAM RD.

CHESHIRE FOREST CT.

HANHAM

ARCHER

GIBSON

JOHNSON VS.

SMITH GDS.

Cemetery

23 Westfield Cottage

BRANSTON

Branston Hall

Branston PARK

BRANSTON PARK

ROAD

HIGH ST.

BRAY'S BUSINESS CENTRE

VILLA

4

field m

Peggy's Holt

Branston Old Hall

Wheel Ho.

Springfield

RECTORY LA.

CHURCH RD.

CHAPEL

SILVER ST.

MELVILLE

THACKERS

LA.

67

WATERWHEEL

Hare Wood

5

HALL

LANE

TOLLY

MEERE

ROAD

6

366

Ash Holt

Fox Covert

Giles' Gorse

BLOXHOLM

7

A **B** **C** **D** **E**

500   01   02

Chapel Hill

Mere Hall

LANE

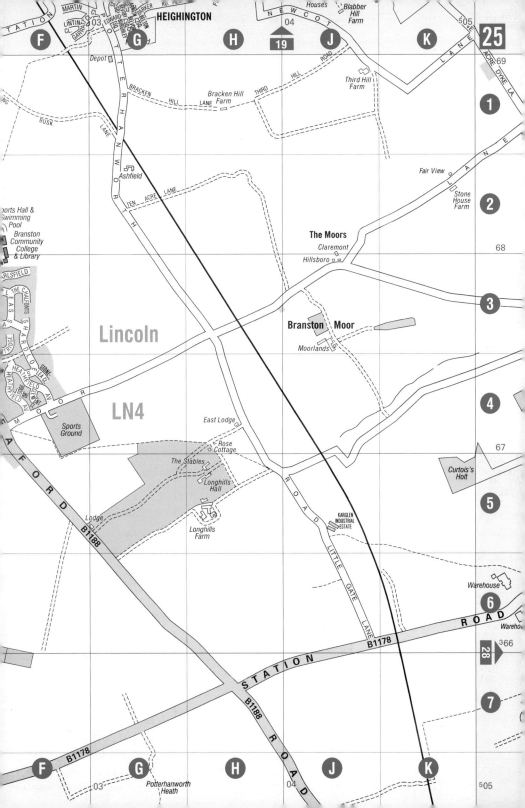

26

495 · A · 96 WASHDIKE · B · 96 · C · D · 97 · E

1

MEADOW CL

Pump Drain

Witham

Depot

Hykeham Bridge

22

The Sidney Hall Memorial Play. Field

CAIRNS WY.
HOBART CL.
BRIS.
BAND
CL.
MELBOURNE
LYTLE-JANE CL.
DARWIN CL.

FIR TREE AV.
REDWOOD
Cen.
WOOD
CLOSE
WAY

Works

STATION

Station Fm.
Depot
SOMER.
VILLE CT. SOMERVILLE
GARTH GREENS

Nursery

Station Road Farm

2

The Beck

River

LN6

365

WADDINGTON LOW FIELDS

MEADOW LANE

3

BRANT

SOMERTON GATE LANE

Nursery

ROAD

Lincoln

Stable Close

HILL

TOP

LANE

VIKING

STAP.

INSET

THE AVENUE

A46

Ash Holt

SHEEPWALK

Sheepwalks Cott.

Sheepwalks Farm

New Close

4

The Dovecot

63

HALFWAY RDBT.

Halfway Houses

LN6

GIBSON NETTLETON DR.
CHESHIRE LA.
HANNAH CRES. NETTLETON DR.

LANE

GREEN

Lincoln

5

Works

Works

ROAD

CAMP

Airfield (disused)

6

Witham St. Hughs Prim. School

SQUIRREL LA.
DOE CL.
WARREN CL.
GINN. CL.
R.BRIDGE 'GRN'.
ROBIN CL.
ELDER CRES.
WINTUM WY.
LIVERPOOL CHASE
FOX HOLLOW

GREEN

LANE

62

Firholt Plantation

RCK. WS. WK.
WRKS. ROK.
GREENWICH CRES.
WHIM DR.
WOORHEN CL.
HEDGEROW
PINES
TAIL
SORREL RD.
ROSE HIP WK.
OAK TREE CL.
PENROD
PATCH RD.
SATTERLEY DR.
SATTERY CL.
ROE CL.
KINNET WK.

Play's. grd.

WITHAM ST. HUGHS

Sewage Works

LN5

7

Thurlby Moor

MOOR

CAMP

NORTON LANE

Greengate Farm

89

A · B · 490 · C

HARMSTON

Highfie Farm

VICARAGE

Milton House Farm

The Grange

BLACKSMITH HILL
SCHOOL LA.†
CHAPEL LA.
HIGH STREET
TOP

STATION ROAD

CHURCH

Bottom Park

Sewage Works

Harmston Hall

Harmston Park

WALLER
HARMSTON PK.
RIDGE HARMSTON
WY. AV.

PARK

COCKBURN WY.
CRES.

Round Plantations

Oak Holt

Belt Plantation

CLOSE THORNOLD

D · 97 · **E**

HARMSTON

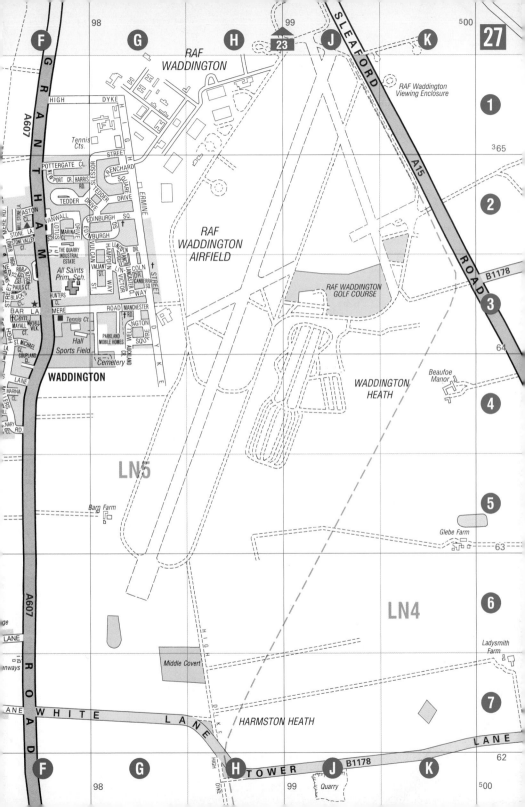

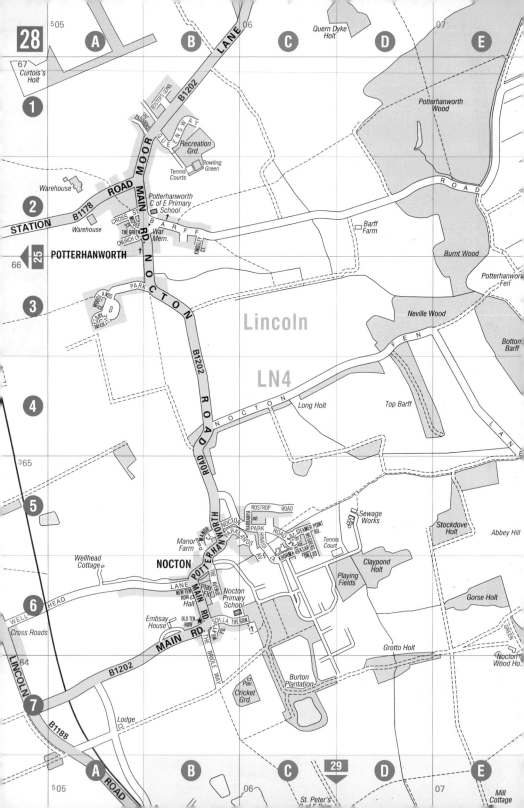

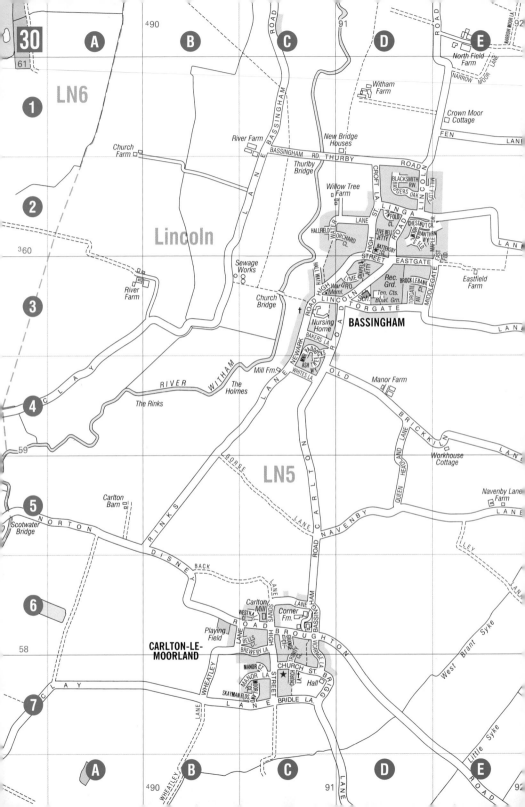

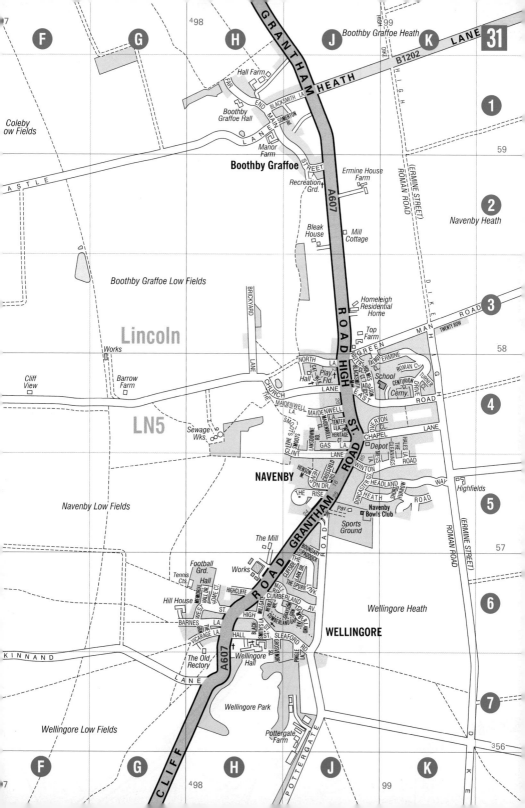

INDEX

Including Streets, Places & Areas, Hospitals & Hospices, Industrial Estates,
Selected Flats & Walkways, Stations and Selected Places of Interest.

HOW TO USE THIS INDEX

1. Each street name is followed by its Postcode District, then by its Locality abbreviation(s) and then by its map reference;
   e.g. **Aberporth Dr.** LN6: Lin . . . .6F **15** is in the LN6 Postcode District and the Lincoln Locality and is to be found in square 6F on page **15**.
   The page number is shown in bold type.

2. A strict alphabetical order is followed in which Av., Rd., St., etc. (though abbreviated) are read in full and as part of the street name;
   e.g. **Ash Tree Av.** appears after **Ashton's Ct.** but before **Ashtree Way**

3. Streets and a selection of flats and walkways too small to be shown on the maps, appear in the index with the thoroughfare to which it is connected shown in brackets; e.g. **Appleby Ho.** LN6: Lin . . . .7K **15** (off Carrington Dr.)

4. Addresses that are in more than one part are referred to as not continuous.

5. Places and areas are shown in the index in BLUE TYPE and the map reference is to the actual map square in which the town centre or area is located and not to the place name shown on the map; e.g. BALDERTON 4H 37

6. An example of a selected place of interest is **Lincolnshire Road Transport Mus.** 2H 21

7. An example of a station is **Collingham Station (Rail)** 4J 33

8. An example of a hospital or hospice is **LINCOLN COUNTY HOSPITAL** 2H 17

9. Map references for entries that appear on large scale page **38** are shown first, with small scale map references shown in brackets;
   e.g. **Abbey Pl.** LN2: Lin 4E **38** (3G **17**)

GENERAL ABBREVIATIONS

App. : Approach	**Gdn.** : Garden	**Pde.** : Parade
Arc. : Arcade	**Gdns.** : Gardens	**Pk.** : Park
Av. : Avenue	**Gth.** : Garth	**Pas.** : Passage
Blvd. : Boulevard	**Ga.** : Gate	**Pl.** : Place
Bri. : Bridge	**Gt.** : Great	**Ri.** : Rise
Bldgs. : Buildings	**Grn.** : Green	**Rd.** : Road
Bus. : Business	**Gro.** : Grove	**Rdbt.** : Roundabout
Cvn. : Caravan	**Hgts.** : Heights	**Shop.** : Shopping
Cen. : Centre	**Ho.** : House	**Sth.** : South
Circ. : Circle	**Ind.** : Industrial	**Sq.** : Square
Cl. : Close	**Info.** : Information	**St.** : Street
Cnr. : Corner	**La.** : Lane	**Ter.** : Terrace
Cott. : Cottage	**Lit.** : Little	**Trad.** : Trading
Cotts. : Cottages	**Lwr.** : Lower	**Up.** : Upper
Ct. : Court	**Mnr.** : Manor	**Vw.** : View
Cres. : Crescent	**Mkt.** : Market	**Vs.** : Villas
Cft. : Croft	**Mdw.** : Meadow	**Vis.** : Visitors
Dr. : Drive	**Mdws.** : Meadows	**Wlk.** : Walk
E. : East	**M.** : Mews	**W.** : West
Est. : Estate	**Mt.** : Mount	**Yd.** : Yard
Fld. : Field	**Mus.** : Museum	
Flds. : Fields	**Nth.** : North	

LOCALITY ABBREVIATIONS

Bald : **Balderton**	Fis : **Fiskerton**	Ris : **Riseholme**
Barn W : **Barnby in the Willows**	Harby : **Harby**	Sax : **Saxilby**
Bass : **Bassingham**	Hard : **Hardwick**	Scot : **Scothern**
Bath : **Bathley**	Harm : **Harmston**	Skel : **Skellingthorpe**
Best : **Besthorpe**	Hawt : **Hawton**	S Car : **South Carlton**
Blank : **Blankney**	H'ton : **Heighington**	S Hyk : **South Hykeham**
Booth G : **Boothby Graffoe**	Holm : **Holme**	S Mus : **South Muskham**
Brac B : **Bracebridge Heath**	Kel : **Kelham**	Stain L : **Stainton by Langworth**
Bran : **Branston**	Lang W : **Langton by Wragby**	Swin : **Swinderby**
Bro : **Broadholme**	L'worth : **Langworth**	Thor : **Thorney**
Brox : **Broxholme**	Lin : **Lincoln**	Thpe : **Thorpe**
Bur : **Burton**	Lit C : **Little Carlton**	T Hill : **Thorpe-on-the-Hill**
B Wat : **Burton Waters**	Meth : **Metheringham**	Thurl : **Thurlby**
Can : **Canwick**	Nav : **Navenby**	Wad : **Waddington**
Carl M : **Carlton-le-Moorland**	Nett : **Nettleham**	Wash : **Washingborough**
C Will : **Cherry Willingham**	N'wark T : **Newark-on-Trent**	Well : **Wellingore**
Codd : **Coddington**	New B : **New Balderton**	Welt : **Welton**
Coll : **Collingham**	Noct : **Nocton**	Whi : **Whisby**
Dodd : **Doddington**	N Gre : **North Greetwell**	Wint : **Winthorpe**
D Noo : **Drisney Nook**	N Hyk : **North Hykeham**	With S : **Witham St Hughs**
Dunh : **Dunholme**	N Mus : **North Muskham**	Wrag : **Wragby**
Duns : **Dunston**	Pott : **Potterhanworth**	
Farn : **Farndon**	Ree : **Reepham**	

A

	Abbot St. LN5: Lin 7B **38** (5E **16**)	Abingdon Cl. LN6: Lin 1G **21**
	Abbott's Way NG24: N'wark T 6F **35**	Acacia Av. LN5: Wad 6D **22**
	Abel Smith Gdns. LN4: Bran 4E **24**	Acacia Rd. NG24: New B 3H **37**
Abbey Pl. LN2: Lin 4E **38** (3G **17**)	Aberporth Dr. LN6: Lin 6F **15**	Acer Cl. LN6: Lin 7H **15**
Abbey St. LN2: Lin 4D **38** (3G **17**)	Abingdon Av. LN6: Lin 1G **21**	Acer Ct. LN6: Lin 7H **15**

Acorn Cl. LN5: Lin 7D 16
  NG24: New B 3G 37
Acre Dyke La. LN4: Bran 7K 19
Adam Cl. LN6: Lin 7H 15
Addison Cl. LN5: Nav 4J 31
Addison Dr. LN2: Lin 7H 11
Adelaide Cl. LN5: Wad 1D 26
Admiral Wlk. LN2: Lin 1H 17
Adwalton Cl. NG24: N'wark T 7J 35
Aima Cl. LN2: Nett 1B 12
Ainsdale Cl. NG24: Bald 6J 37
Aisne Cl. LN1: Lin 6E 10
Akeman Dr. LN4: Brac B 5G 23
Akrotiri Sq. LN4: Noct 5C 28
Alabala Cl. LN4: Wash 5E 18
Alabala La. LN4: H'ton 6G 19
Albany St. LN1: Lin 1E 16
Albany Ter. LN1: Lin 2D 22
Albert Av. NG24: Bald 4G 37
Albert Cres. LN1: Lin 2D 16
Albert St. NG24: N'wark T 1D 36
Albert Ter. LN5: Lin 6D 16
Albion Cl. LN1: Lin 7C 10
Albion Cres. LN1: Lin 7C 10
Albion St. NG24: N'wark T 7D 34
Alconbury Cl. LN6: Lin 1G 21
Alder Cl. LN6: N Hyk 5K 21
  NG24: New B 3G 37
Aldergrove Cl. LN6: Lin 7G 15
Aldergrove Cres. LN6: Lin 7G 15
Alderman's Wlk. LN1: Lin 1A 38 (2C 16)
Alderney Way LN6: N Hyk 6A 22
Alders, The LN2: Scot 7G 5
Aldreth Vs. LN1: Lin 1B 38
Alexander Av. NG24: N'wark T 3F 35
Alexander Cl. LN4: Meth 5K 29
Alexander Wlk. LN2: Lin 7K 11
Alexandra Ter. LN1: Lin 2A 38 (2E 16)
Alexandre Av. LN6: N Hyk 6K 21
Alford Mill Cl. LN6: N Hyk 7H 21
Alfred Av. LN4: Meth 5G 29
Alfred St. LN5: Lin 7A 38 (5E 16)
Allandale Cl. LN1: Lin 5D 10
Allandale Vw. LN1: Lin 5D 10
Allenby Bus. Village LN3: Lin 2K 17
Allenby Rd. LN2: Lin 2K 17
  LN3: Lin 2K 17
Alliance St. NG24: N'wark T 5E 34
Allison Pl. LN1: Lin 2D 16
Allison St. LN1: Lin 2D 16
All Saints La. LN2: Nett 1B 12
Allwood Rd. LN2: Dunh 3D 4
Almond Av. LN4: H'ton 7G 19
  LN6: Lin 6A 16
Almond Cl. LN1: Sax 2F 9
Almond Ct. LN6: Lin 6A 16
Almond Cres. LN4: H'ton 7G 19
  LN5: Wad 6D 22
  LN6: Lin 6A 16
Almond Gro. LN6: Skel 2E 14
Almond Ho. LN6: Lin 6A 16
Almond Wlk. LN5: Well 6H 31
Alness Cl. LN6: Lin 6F 15
Altham Ter. LN5: Lin 6E 16
  LN6: Lin 7D 16
Althea Ter. LN3: Ree 4H 13
Alumnia Ct. LN6: Lin 7A 16
Alvey Rd. NG24: Bald 4J 37
Alvis Cl. LN4: Brac B 5F 23
Amble Cl. LN1: Lin 5E 10
Ambleside Pk. LN6: N Hyk 6K 21
Ancaster Av. LN2: Lin 1H 17
Ancaster Cl. LN3: C Will 7G 13
Ancholme Cl. LN1: Lin 5D 10
Anchor Cl. LN5: Lin 7A 38 (4E 16)
Anchor St. LN5: Lin 7B 38 (4E 16)
Anderby Cl. LN6: Lin 1K 21
Anderby Dr. LN6: Lin 1K 21
Anderson Cl. LN2: Dunh 4D 4
Anderson Cl. NG24: Bald 5F 37
Anderson La. LN1: Lin 7F 11
Andover Cl. LN6: Lin 6F 15
Anglesey Cl. LN6: Lin 7G 15
Anson Cl. LN6: Skel 2E 14
Antrim Rd. LN5: Lin 5D 22
Anzio Cl. LN1: Lin 6E 10
Anzio Cres. LN1: Lin 6E 10

Anzio Ter. LN1: Lin 6E 10
Anzio Wlk. LN1: Lin 6E 10
Apley Cl. LN2: Lin 5G 11
Appian Way LN4: Brac B 5G 23
Apple Av. NG24: Bald 6K 37
Appleby Cl. NG24: N'wark T 7H 35
Appleby Ho. *LN6: Lin* *7K 15*
  (off Carrington Dr.)
Appleby Way LN6: Lin 6F 15
Apple Cl. LN1: H'ton 6G 19
Apple Gth. LN5: Lin 3D 22
Appleton Ga. NG24: N'wark T 7E 34
Apple Tree Cl. LN4: Meth 4H 29
Arabis Cl. LN2: Lin 5J 11
Arboretum Av. LN2: Lin 3G 17
Arboretum Vw. LN2: Lin 3G 17
Arcade, The NG24: N'wark T 7D 34
Archer Rd. LN4: Bran 3E 24
Archer St. LN5: Lin 7D 38 (4F 17)
Archway Dr. LN8: Wrag 4F 7
Arden Moor Way LN6: N Hyk 7H 21
Arlington Ct. LN4: Wash 5D 18
Arnhem Cl. LN1: Lin 6E 10
Arras Cl. LN1: Lin 7E 10
Arthur St. LN5: Lin 5F 17
Arthur Taylor St. LN1: Lin 3D 16
Ascot Way LN6: N Hyk 7F 21
Ashby Av. LN6: Lin 7K 15
Ashby Cl. LN5: Wad 6D 22
Ash Cl. LN6: Lin 6J 15
Ashdale Cl. LN4: Meth 4G 29
Asheridge LN4: Bran 3F 25
Ashfield Grange LN1: Sax 2D 8
Ashfield St. LN2: Lin 3H 17
Ash Gro. LN3: C Will 1F 19
  LN6: N Hyk 5K 21
Ash Holt Cl. LN3: Fis 3K 19
Ashing La. LN2: Dunh 3F 5
  (not continuous)
Ash La. LN5: Wad 3E 26
Ashley Ct. LN5: Lin 7D 16
Ashlin Gro. LN1: Lin 3A 38 (2D 16)
Ash Rd. NG24: N'wark T 4D 36
Ashton's Ct. LN5: Lin 7B 38 (5E 16)
Ash Tree Av. LN2: Nett 2C 12
Ashtree Way LN5: Bass 4C 30
Ashworth Cl. LN6: Lin 2K 21
  NG24: N'wark T 7H 35
Asterby Cl. LN2: Lin 6G 11
Aster Cl. LN2: Lin 5J 11
Aston Cl. LN5: Wad 2F 27
Astral Way LN6: N Hyk 6G 21
Astwick Rd. LN6: Lin 2A 22
Atwater Cl. LN2: Lin 6K 11
Atwater Ct. LN2: Lin 6K 11
Atwater Gro. LN2: Lin 6K 11
Auborne Av. LN2: Lin 6F 11
Auden Cl. LN2: Lin 1G 17
Austen Wlk. LN2: Lin 7J 11
Autumn Cft. Rd. NG24: N'wark T 6H 35
Avenue, The LN1: Lin 4A 38 (3E 16)
  LN4: Noct 6B 28
  LN6: Swin 4A 26
  NG24: N'wark T 1F 37
Avenue Ter. LN1: Lin 3A 38 (2E 16)
Avocet Cl. LN6: Lin 6H 15
Avon Cl. LN6: N Hyk 5A 22
Avondale LN6: N Hyk 6G 21
Avondale St. LN2: Lin 3G 17
Ayam Cl. LN2: Welt 2C 4
Aylesby Cl. LN1: Lin 6F 11
Aynsley Cl. LN6: Lin 1G 21
Aynsley Rd. LN6: Lin 1F 21
Azalea Rd. LN2: Lin 5J 11

Bailgate LN1: Lin 2C 38 (2F 17)
Baines Av. NG24: New B 4H 37
Bain St. LN1: Lin 5D 10
Bakehosue Ct LN3: L'worth 4C 6
Baker Cres. LN1: Lin 7J 15
Bakers La. LN5: Bass 3C 30
Bakewell Cl. NG24: New B 5G 37
Bakewell Ho. NG24: Bald 5G 37
Bakewell M. LN6: N Hyk 6K 21
BALDERTON 4H 37
Balderton Ga. NG24: N'wark T 7E 34
Balderton La. NG24: Codd 2K 37
Ballerini Way LN1: Sax 3G 9
Balmoral Cl. LN8: Wrag 4G 7
Balmoral Dr. NG24: N'wark T 7J 35
Balmoral Ho. LN2: Lin 5H 11
Bamford Cl. LN6: N Hyk 5J 21
Bancroft Rd. NG24: N'wark T 2F 37
Bangor Cl. LN5: Lin 4C 22
Banks Lodge *LN6: Lin* *3D 16*
  (off The Pavilions Student Village)
Bank St. LN2: Lin 5C 38 (3F 17)
Baptist La. NG23: Coll 4G 33
Bardney Cl. LN2: Lin 1K 21
Bardney Rd. LN4: Wash 5K 19
  LN8: Wrag 5F 7
Barff Rd. LN4: Pott 2B 28
Barfields La. LN2: Scot 3H 13
  LN3: Scot 3H 13
Bar Ga. NG24: N'wark T 6D 34
Bargate LN5: Lin 6E 16
Barker's Ct. LN5: Lin 5D 38
Barkstone Cl. NG24: Bald 5G 37
Barkston Gdns. LN2: Lin 6H 11
Bar La. LN5: Wad 3F 27
Barley Cl. LN4: Meth 5G 29
Barleyfield Cl. LN4: H'ton 6E 18
Barley Way NG24: N'wark T 3F 35
BARLINGS 7E 6
Barlings Cl. LN3: L'worth 5C 6
  LN6: Lin 7K 15
Barlings La. LN3: L'worth 5C 6
Barnby Ga. NG24: N'wark T 7E 34
Barnby Rd.
  NG24: Bald, Barn W, N'wark T ...1F 37
Barnes La. LN5: Well 6H 31
Barnes Wallis Ct. LN2: Welt 1C 4
Barnfield Rd. NG23: Coll 3J 33
Barratt's Cl. LN2: Lin 1E 38 (1G 17)
Barrett Gro. LN2: Dunh 3E 4
Barrons Cl. LN3: C Will 6G 13
Barrows Ga. NG24: N'wark T 4F 35
BASSINGHAM 2D 30
Bassingham Cres. LN2: Lin 6F 11
Bassingham Rd. LN5: Carl M 6C 30
  LN5: Thurl 1C 30
Bathley La. NG23: Bath 1A 34
  (not continuous)
  NG23: N Mus 4A 32
Bath Rd. LN4: Brac B 3H 23
Bathurst St. LN2: Lin 2K 17
Battersby Cl. LN5: Bass 2D 30
Bawtry Cl. LN1: Lin 6F 15
Bayford Dr. NG24: N'wark T 1J 37
Bayons Ho. *LN6: Lin* *7K 15*
  (off Carrington Dr.)
Baywood Cl. LN6: Lin 5G 15
Beacon Hgts. NG24: N'wark T 7H 35
Beacon Hill Rd. NG24: N'wark T ...7E 34
Beaconsfield Dr. NG24: Codd 5K 37
Beacon Ter. NG24: N'wark T 7E 34
Beacon Way NG24: N'wark T 7H 35
Beast Mkt. Hill NG24: N'wark T 6D 34
Beaufort Cl. LN5: Lin 5K 11
Beaufort Rd. LN2: Lin 5K 11
BEAUMOND HOUSE COMMUNITY HOSPICE
  ....1D 36
Beaumont Fee LN1: Lin 4B 38 (3E 16)
  (not continuous)
Beaumont Wlk. NG24: N'wark T 5F 35
  (not continuous)
Beaver Cl. LN6: Skel 1E 14
Becke Cl. LN3: C Will 1G 19
Becket Cl. LN4: Wash 5F 19
Beckhall LN2: Welt 2C 4
Beckhead Cvn. Site LN6: N Hyk ...6G 21
Beck Hill LN3: Ree 5H 13

B

Back La. LN2: Scot 7H 5
  LN4: Duns 1F 29
  LN4: H'ton 7G 19
  LN5: Carl M 6B 30
Badgers Cl. LN6: Skel 1E 14
Badgers Oak LN5: Bass 2D 30
Baggholme Rd. LN2: Lin 5E 38 (3G 17)
Baildon Cres. LN6: N Hyk 4A 22
Bailey Rd. NG24: N'wark T 3D 36

Beckingham Rd.—Burghley Rd.

Beckingham Rd. NG24: Codd 6K **35**
Beck La. LN2: Dunh 3F **5**
LN4: H'ton 6G **19**
Beckside LN2: Nett 2B **12**
LN6: N Hyk 7K **21**
Bede Ho. Ct. NG24: N'wark T 7E **34**
Bede Ho. La. NG24: N'wark T 7E **34**
Bedford St. LN1: Lin 2D **16**
Beech Av. LN2: Nett 2A **12**
NG24: N'wark T 3D **36**
Beech Cl. LN2: Dunh 4E **4**
LN2: Scot 1G **13**
LN4: Brac B 5G **23**
Beech Ct. LN5: Lin 2D **22**
Beech Cft. Cl. LN6: S Hyk 7F **21**
Beech Rd. LN4: Bran 3C **24**
Beech St. LN5: Lin 2D **22**
Beefield, The LN2: Lin 6B **12**
Beeston Rd. NG24: N'wark T 2F **37**
Beevor St. LN6: Lin 7A **38** (3C **16**)
Belgrave Ct. LN4: Wash 5D **18**
Belgravia Cl. LN6: Lin 4J **15**
Belle Vue Rd. LN1: Lin 2A **38** (2E **16**)
Belle Vue Ter. LN1: Lin 2A **38** (2E **16**)
Bellflower Cl. LN2: Lin 5J **11**
Bell Gro. LN6: Lin 1C **22**
Bell La. NG23: Coll 4G **33**
Bellmond Cl. NG24: N'wark T 3D **36**
Bells Ct. LN5: Carl M 6C **30**
Bell's Mdw. LN4: H'ton 7G **19**
Bell St. LN5: Lin 6E **16**
Bellwood Grange LN3: C Will 6G **13**
Belmont St. LN2: Lin 3H **17**
Belton Av. LN6: Lin 1K **21**
Belton Pk. Dr. LN6: N Hyk 7K **21**
Belton Sq. LN4: H'ton 7G **19**
Belvedere Ho. LN2: Lin 5F **11**
Belvoir Cl. LN5: Wad 6D **22**
Belvoir Cres. NG24: N'wark T 2E **36**
Belvoir Pl. NG24: Bald 5G **37**
Belvoir Rd. NG24: Bald 5G **37**
Belvoir Sq. LN4: H'ton 7G **19**
Benbow Way LN1: Lin 7C **10**
Bendigo Cl. LN1: Lin 6D **10**
Bennington Cl. LN6: Lin 7K **15**
Benson Cl. LN6: Lin 1G **21**
Benson Cres. LN6: Lin 1G **21**
Bentinck Rd. NG24: N'wark T 2D **36**
Bentinck Sq. LN2: Lin 3H **17**
Bentinck St. LN2: Lin 3H **17**
Bentley Dr. LN4: Brac B 4F **23**
Bentley Way LN4: Meth 4G **29**
Beresford Dr. LN2: Scot 1H **13**
Berkeley Av. LN6: Lin 4A **22**
Berkeley Ct. LN4: Wash 4D **18**
Berkeley Dr. LN6: Lin 4A **22**
Bernard St. LN2: Lin 3H **17**
Besthorpe Rd. NG23: Best 1G **33**
Beswick Cl. LN6: Lin 7H **15**
Betula Gro. LN6: Lin 7H **15**
Bevercotes Cl. NG24: N'wark T 2C **36**
Beverley Gro. LN6: N Hyk 4K **21**
Bilsby Cl. LN2: Lin 6G **11**
Bilton Cl. NG24: Bald 6H **37**
Binbrook Cl. LN6: Lin 7H **15**
Birch Cl. LN4: Bran 3D **24**
LN6: N Hyk 5K **21**
Birches, The LN6: S Hyk 7F **21**
Birch Rd. NG24: New B 3G **37**
BIRCHWOOD 6G **15**
Birchwood Av. LN6: Lin 6G **15**
Birchwood Cen. LN6: Lin 6G **15**
Birchwood Community & Leisure Cen. 6G **15**
Birchwood Grange *LN6: Lin* *5J* ***15***
(off Meadowlake Cl.)
Birds Holt Cl. LN6: Skel 3E **14**
Birkdale LN5: Lin 6D **22**
Birkdale Cl. LN4: H'ton 5G **19**
Bishop Alexander Ct. NG24: N'wark T 1C **36**
Bishop Cl. LN2: Dunh 3F **5**
Bishop King Ct. LN5: Lin 5F **17**
BISHOP'S BRIDGE 6A **10**
Bishop's Pl. LN2: Welt 2B **4**
Bishops Rd. LN2: Lin 1J **17**
Bittern Way LN6: Lin 6H **15**
Blackberry Cl. LN6: S Hyk 7F **21**
Blackbourn Cl. NG23: Coll 3J **33**
Blackbourn Rd. LN6: Lin 1C **22**
Blackbrook Rd. NG24: N'wark T 6H **35**
Blackfriars Ct. LN2: Lin 7A **12**
Blackfriars Rd. LN2: Lin 7A **12**
Blackfriars Wlk. LN2: Lin 7A **12**
Black Horse Dr. LN6: S Hyk 7E **20**
Black La. LN6: Dodd, Whi 1A **20**
Black's Cl. LN5: Wad 3F **27**
Blacksmith Ct. LN4: Meth 4H **29**
Blacksmith La. LN4: H'ton 6G **19**
LN5: Booth G 1H **31**
LN5: Harm 7E **26**
LN6: T Hill 7B **20**
Blacksmith M. LN5: Nav 4J **31**
Blacksmith Rd. LN3: Fis 1K **19**
Blacksmith Row LN5: Bass 2D **30**
Blacksmith's La. LN5: Well 6H **31**
Blackthorn Cl. LN2: Lin 5J **11**
Blackthorn Ct. LN6: S Hyk 7F **21**
Blackthorne Cl. NG24: New B 3G **37**
Blackthorn La. LN3: C Will 6G **13**
BLANKNEY 7H **29**
Blankney Cl. LN1: Sax 2D **8**
Blankney Cres. LN2: Lin 5F **11**
Blatherwick Rd. NG24: N'wark T 7H **35**
Blenheim Cl. LN6: Skel 2D **14**
Blenheim Rd. LN1: Lin 2D **16**
Blenheim Sq. LN1: Lin 6E **10**
Blind La. LN5: Wad 3E **26**
Bloxholm La. LN4: Brac B 5H **23**
Bluebell Cl. LN5: Lin 5C **22**
Bluebell Ct. LN4: Brac B 5G **23**
Blyton Cl. LN6: Lin 7G **15**
Blyton Gro. LN6: Lin 7G **15**
Blyton Rd. LN6: Lin 7G **15**
Boar La. NG24: N'wark T 7D **34**
Bobbin La. LN2: Lin 7A **12**
Bodmin Moor Cl. LN6: N Hyk 6H **21**
Bolton Av. LN6: N Hyk 4A **22**
Bona Cl. LN4: Meth 5H **29**
BOOTHBY GRAFFOE 1H **31**
Boscombe Cl. LN6: Lin 1G **21**
Boswell Dr. LN6: Lin 3A **22**
Boswell Gro. LN6: Lin 2K **21**
Bottesford Cl. LN6: Lin 6H **15**
Bottom Row NG24: N'wark T 7F **35**
BOULTHAM 6D **16**
Boultham Av. LN5: Lin 5E **16**
BOULTHAM MOOR 7C **16**
Boultham Pk. Rd. LN6: Lin 7C **16**
Boundary Ct. NG24: N'wark T 1D **36**
Boundary La. LN6: S Hyk 7E **20**
Boundary Paddock LN5: Nav 5J **31**
Boundary Rd. NG24: N'wark T 1C **36**
Boundary St. LN5: Lin 1D **22**
Bourne Cl. LN6: Lin 2B **22**
Bowbridge La. NG24: New B, N'wark T 4E **36**
Bowbridge Rd. NG24: N'wark T 1E **36**
Bowden Dr. LN6: Lin 2A **22**
Bower Cvn. Site NG24: N'wark T 6C **34**
Bower Ct. NG24: N'wark T 6E **34**
BRACEBRIDGE 1D **22**
BRACEBRIDGE HEATH 3F **23**
BRACEBRIDGE LOW FIELDS 4D **22**
Bracken Hill La. LN4: H'ton 1G **25**
Bradbury Av. LN5: Lin 5C **22**
Braemer Rd. NG23: Coll 4H **33**
Bramble Cl. LN2: Welt 1C **4**
Bramble Ct. LN2: Nett 2D **12**
LN4: Brac B 5G **23**
Brambles, The LN3: C Will 7D **12**
Bramley Ct. LN6: Lin 3K **21**
Brancaster Dr. LN6: Lin 6C **16**
Brandon Cl. NG24: Bald 4J **37**
BRANSTON 4E **24**
Branston Bus. Pk. LN4: Bran 3C **24**
Branston Cl. LN6: Lin 3B **22**
NG24: Wint 1H **35**
BRANSTON MOOR 3J **25**
Branston Rd. LN4: Bran, H'ton 2E **24**
Brantley M. LN5: Lin 2D **22**
Brant Rd. LN5: Wad 3B **26**
Brattleby Cres. LN2: Lin 6F **11**
Brayford Ct. LN1: Lin 3A **38**
Brayford Quays LN1: Lin 4A **38** (3E **16**)
Brayford St. LN5: Lin 5B **38** (3E **16**)
Brayford Way LN6: Lin 4A **38** (3D **16**)
Brayford Wharf E. LN5: Lin 6B **38** (4E **16**)
Brayford Wharf Nth. LN1: Lin 4A **38** (3E **16**)
Brays Bus. Cen. LN4: Bran 4E **24**
Brecon Cl. LN6: Lin 7F **15**
Breedon Dr. LN1: Lin 6D **10**
Brewer's Wharf NG24: N'wark T 6D **34**
Brewery La. LN5: Carl M 6C **30**
Brewhouse, The NG24: N'wark T 7D **34**
Briar Cl. LN6: Lin 5G **15**
LN6: S Hyk 7F **21**
Brickyard La. LN5: Nav 3H **31**
Bridge Pl. LN1: Sax 3F **9**
Bridge St. LN1: Sax 3E **8**
LN2: Nett 2B **12**
NG24: N'wark T 7D **34**
Bridge Wlk. LN1: B Wat 7J **9**
Bridle La. LN5: Carl M 7C **30**
Bridle Way LN8: Wrag 3H **7**
Bridle Way, The LN4: Noct 6B **28**
Brigg Cl. LN6: Lin 1G **21**
Brigg Gro. LN6: Lin 1G **21**
Brigg La. LN5: Carl M 7C **30**
Brigg Rd. LN2: Ris 1E **10**
Brinkhall Way LN2: Welt 1C **4**
Brinkle Spring La. LN4: H'ton 6J **19**
Brisbane Cl. LN5: Wad 1C **26**
Brisbane Ct. NG24: Bald 4H **37**
Bristol Cl. NG24: Codd 6J **35**
Bristol Dr. LN6: Lin 6C **16**
Brittania Ct. NG24: N'wark T 7C **34**
Broad Dale Cl. LN2: Scot 1H **13**
Broadgate LN2: Lin 5D **38** (3F **17**)
BROADHOLME 5E **8**
Broadholme Rd. LN1: Sax 4E **8**
Broadway LN2: Lin 7F **11**
LN4: Brac B 4G **23**
LN6: N Hyk 4K **21**
Broadway Cl. LN2: Lin 7F **11**
Brockenhurst Cl. LN6: Lin 7F **15**
Brocklebank Cl. LN5: Bass 3D **30**
Bromley Av. NG24: N'wark T 2E **36**
Brooke Cl. NG24: Bald 3H **37**
Brookfield Av. LN2: Nett 1C **12**
Brookfield Cl. LN6: Skel 1E **14**
Brooklands Cl. LN6: Lin 7G **15**
NG23: Coll 3H **33**
Brooklands Way LN6: Lin 7G **15**
Brook St. LN2: Lin 5D **38** (3F **17**)
Broome Cl. NG24: New B 3F **37**
Broomhill LN6: Lin 6G **15**
Brough Cl. LN6: Lin 7G **15**
Broughton Dr. NG24: N'wark T 3C **36**
Broughton Gdns. LN5: Lin 4D **22**
NG24: Bald 4J **37**
Broughton Rd. LN5: Carl M 6C **30**
Browning Dr. LN2: Lin 6H **11**
Browning Rd. NG24: Bald 3J **37**
Brownlow's Hill NG24: Codd 6K **35**
Brown Wood La. NG23: Thor 7A **8**
Broxburn Pk. LN6: S Hyk 7E **20**
Broxholme Gdns. LN2: Lin 5F **11**
Broxholme La. LN1: Brox, Bur, Sax 1J **9**
LN1: Sax 1F **9**
Bruce Cl. LN2: Lin 7G **11**
Bruce Rd. LN2: Lin 7G **11**
Brumby Cres. LN5: Wad 2E **26**
Brunel Bus. Pk. NG24: N'wark T 6F **35**
Brunel Ct. NG24: N'wark T 5G **35**
Brunel Dr. NG24: N'wark T 6F **35**
Brunel Dr. Workshops NG24: N'wark T 3G **35**
Bryans Cl. NG24: Codd 5J **35**
Buchanan St. LN1: Lin 5D **10**
Buck Cl. LN2: Lin 7K **11**
Buckfast Rd. LN1: Lin 7E **10**
Buckingham Ho. LN2: Lin 5G **11**
Bucknall Av. LN6: Lin 7K **15**
Buddleia Dr. LN4: Bran 3D **24**
Buller Cl. NG23: Coll 3J **33**
Bullingham Rd. LN2: Lin 6K **11**
Bullpit Rd. NG24: Bald 4H **37**
Bungalows, The LN3: Lin 2C **18**
Bunkers Hill LN2: Lin 7K **11**
Bure Cl. LN6: Lin 4K **21**
Burghley Cl. LN6: Lin 5J **15**
Burghley Pk. Cl. LN6: N Hyk 6K **21**
Burghley Rd. LN6: Lin 5J **15**

Burghley Sq. LN4: H'ton 7G 19
Burland Ct. LN4: Bran 3E 24
   LN4: Wash 4D 18
Burneside Cl. LN2: Lin 5H 11
Burnmoor Ct. LN6: Lin 5G 15
Burns Gdns. LN2: Lin 7J 11
BURTON 3B 10
Burton Cliffe LN1: Lin 6D 10
Burtonfield Cl. LN3: C Will 7G 13
Burton La. End LN1: B Wat 6H 9
   (not continuous)
Burton M. LN1: Lin .7E 10
   LN4: Wash 5F 19
Burton Ridge LN1: Lin 6D 10
Burton Rd. LN1: Lin 1B 38 (7E 10)
BURTON WATERS .7J 9
Burwell Cl. LN2: Lin 5G 11
Butchers La. LN4: H'ton 7G 19
Butchery Ct. LN2: Lin 4C 38 (3F 17)
Buttercup Cl. NG24: New B 3G 37
Buttergate, The NG24: N'wark T 7D 34
   (off Market Pl.)
Buttermere Cl. LN6: Lin 5H 15
Buttery Cl. LN6: Lin 3K 21
Byland Cl. LN1: Lin 7A 12
Byron Av. LN2: Lin .7G 11
Byron Cl. NG24: N'wark T 2E 36
Byron Ct. NG24: Bald 5J 37

C

Cabourne Av. LN2: Lin 6H 11
Cabourne Ct. LN2: Lin 6H 11
Cade Cl. LN2: Scot .7G 5
Cadwell Cl. LN6: Lin 7G 15
Caenby St. LN1: Lin 7D 10
Cafferata Way NG24: N'wark T 6G 35
Cairns Way LN5: Wad 7C 22
Caistor Cl. LN6: Lin 7G 15
Caistor Dr. LN4: Brac B 3G 23
Caistor Rd. LN6: Lin 7G 15
Calder Rd. LN5: Lin 5C 22
Cambrai Cl. LN1: Lin 6E 10
Cambrian Way LN6: N Hyk 7H 21
Cambridge Av. LN1: Lin 1D 16
Cambridge Dr. LN4: Wash 5E 18
Cambridge Mdws. NG24: N'wark T 7J 35
Camdale La. NG24: Bald 6K 37
Camdon Cl. LN5: Lin 4D 22
Cameron La. NG24: Bald 7K 37
Camp Rd. LN6: With S 6A 26
Campus Way LN1: Lin 3D 16
   LN6: Lin 3D 16
Camwood Cres. LN6: Lin 5G 15
Canberra Sq. LN5: Wad 3G 27
Canberra Way LN6: Skel 2E 14
Cannon Cl. NG24: N'wark T 6J 35
Cannon Stevens Cl. NG23: Coll 4H 33
Cannon St. LN2: Lin 5E 38 (3G 17)
   (not continuous)
Canterbury Dr. LN4: H'ton, Wash 6F 19
Canterbury Rd. LN4: Brac B 3G 23
CANWICK 6H 17
Canwick Av. LN4: Brac B 3F 23
Canwick Hill LN4: Can 6G 17
Canwick Rd. LN4: Wash 6D 18
   LN5: Lin 7D 38 (4F 17)
   (not continuous)
Canwick Rd. Trad. Est.
   LN5: Lin 7E 38 (5G 17)
Capps La. LN5: Wad 3E 26
Cardinal Cl. LN2: Lin 1K 17
Cardinal Hinsley Cl. NG24: N'wark T 4B 36
Cardyke Way LN4: Brac B 7G 23
Carholme Rd. LN1: Lin 4A 38 (2C 16)
Carholme Rdbt. LN1: Lin 7A 10
Carisbrooke Cl. LN6: N Hyk 6K 21
Carline Rd. LN1: Lin 1A 38 (2E 16)
Carlisle Cl. LN6: N Hyk 6K 21
Carlisle Way LN4: Brac B 3H 23
Carlton Blvd. LN2: Lin 1K 17
Carlton Cen. LN2: Lin 7K 11
Carlton Cl. NG24: N'wark T 2E 36
Carlton Ferry La. NG23: Coll 3F 33
Carlton Gro. LN2: Lin 6F 11
CARLTON-LE-MOORLAND 7C 30

Carlton M. LN2: Lin 7K 11
   LN4: Wash 5F 19
Carlton Rd. LN5: Bass 5C 30
   NG24: N'wark T 2D 36
Carlton Sq. LN2: Lin 7K 11
Carlton St. LN1: Lin 1E 16
Carlton Wlk. LN2: Lin 6F 11
Carlyle Wlk. LN2: Lin 7H 11
Carn Cl. LN5: Lin 5D 22
Carnell La. NG24: Bald 7K 37
Carnoustie Dr. LN6: Lin 7F 15
Caroline Rd. LN4: Meth 4J 29
Carral Cl. LN5: Lin .4C 22
Carram Cl. LN1: Lin 6C 10
Carram Way LN1: Lin 6C 10
Carrington Dr. LN6: Lin 7K 15
Carr La. LN6: Dodd 3A 14
   NG23: Harby 7D 8
Carrs, The LN2: Welt 2C 4
Carr St. LN1: Lin 2D 16
Carswell Cl. NG24: N'wark T 2D 36
Carter Ga. NG24: N'wark T 7D 34
Carters Yd. NG24: N'wark T 7D 34
   (off Carter Ga.)
Cassia Grn. LN6: Lin 6G 15
Castle Brewery Ct. NG24: N'wark T 7D 34
Castle Ga. NG24: N'wark T 7D 34
Castle Hill LN1: Lin 2C 38 (2F 17)
   LN5: Booth G 2F 31
Castle Rising NG24: N'wark T 7D 34
   (off Lombard St.)
Castle St. LN1: Lin .1E 16
Castle Vw. Cvn. Pk. NG24: N'wark T 7B 34
Castle Vw. Ct. NG24: N'wark T 6D 34
Cathedral Hgts. LN4: Brac B 3G 23
Cathedral St. LN2: Lin 4D 38 (2F 17)
Cathedral Vw. Ct. LN2: Lin 6H 11
Catkin Way NG24: New B 4F 37
Cat Wlk. LN5: Nav .4J 31
Cavalry Ct. LN4: Meth 4J 29
Cavendish Av. NG24: N'wark T 2E 36
Cavendish M. LN4: Wash 5F 19
Cawthorne Cl. NG23: Coll 3J 33
Caythorpe Ho. LN6: Lin 7K 15
Cecil M. LN1: Lin 1C 38 (1F 17)
Cecil St. LN1: Lin 1B 38 (1E 16)
Cedar Av. LN3: C Will 1F 19
   LN5: Lin 3D 22
   NG24: N'wark T 4F 35
Cedar Cl. LN2: Scot 1H 13
   LN5: Wad 7C 22
Cemetery Rd. LN8: Wrag 4H 7
Centaur Rd. LN6: Lin 4D 16
Centenary Cl. NG24: New B 4G 37
Central Mkt. LN5: Lin 5C 38 (3F 17)
Centurion Cl. LN5: Nav 4K 31
Century La. LN1: Sax 1E 8
Century St. NG24: N'wark T 7E 34
Chain La. NG24: N'wark T 7D 34
Chalet Cvn. Site, The NG23: Bath 4A 32
Chalfonts, The LN4: Bran 3F 25
Chalgrove Way LN6: Lin 4H 15
Chancel Rd. LN2: Welt 2B 4
Chancery Cl. LN6: Lin 2B 22
Chantry Rd. NG24: N'wark T 3D 36
Chapel Cl. LN3: Ree 5H 13
Chapel Jetty LN5: Bass 3D 30
Chapel La. LN1: Lin 1B 38 (1E 16)
   LN2: Nett 2B 12
   LN2: Welt 2B 4
   LN4: Bran 4E 24
   LN4: Duns 2G 29
   LN4: H'ton 7F 19
   LN5: Harm 7E 26
   LN5: Nav 4J 31
   LN6: N Hyk 7K 21
   NG23: N Mus 3C 32
   NG24: Wint 1G 35
Chapel Rd. LN3: Fis 1K 19
   LN4: Bran 4E 24
Chapel Wlk. LN2: Scot 7H 5
Chapel Yd. LN1: Sax 3E 8
   LN4: Bran 4E 24
Chaplin St. LN5: Lin 7B 38 (4E 16)
Chapter Cl. LN2: Welt 1B 4

Charles St. LN5: Lin 7D 38 (4F 17)
   NG24: N'wark T 1F 37
Charles St. W. LN1: Lin 2D 16
Charlesworth Ho. LN6: Lin 3D 16
   (off The Pavilions Student Village)
Charlesworth St. LN6: Lin 3D 16
Charlotte Cl. NG24: N'wark T 7E 34
Chartridge LN4: Bran 3F 25
Chase, The LN4: Meth 3H 29
Chatham Ct. NG24: N'wark T 1D 36
Chatsworth Cl. LN2: Lin 5J 11
Chatsworth Dr. LN6: N Hyk 5J 21
Chatsworth Rd. NG24: N'wark T 3D 36
Chatterton Av. LN1: Lin 5E 10
Chaucer Dr. LN2: Lin 7J 11
Chaucer Rd. NG24: Bald 4J 37
Checkpoint Cl. LN6: Lin 1F 21
Chedburgh Cl. LN6: Lin 1F 21
Chedworth Cl. LN2: Lin 6K 11
Chedworth Rd. LN2: Lin 6K 11
Chelmer Cl. LN6: Lin 3K 21
Chelmsford St. LN5: Lin 7C 38 (4F 17)
Chelsea Cl. LN6: Lin 4H 15
Cheriton Ct. LN5: Lin 7D 38
Cherry Av. LN4: Bran 3D 24
Cherry Blossom Ct. LN6: Lin 6F 15
Cherry Gro. LN6: Lin 6A 16
Cherry Holt LN3: C Will 1G 19
   NG24: N'wark T 3D 36
Cherry Tree Cl. LN6: N Hyk 5K 21
Cherry Tree La. LN2: Nett 2A 12
Cherry Tree Way LN4: Meth 4G 29
CHERRY WILLINGHAM 7G 13
Cheshire Ct. LN4: Bran 3E 24
Cheshire La. LN6: With S 5C 26
Cheshire Rd. LN6: Lin 1E 20
Chesney Rd. LN2: Lin 6K 11
Chester Cl. LN4: Wash 5F 19
Chester Pl. NG24: N'wark T 1C 36
Chestnut Av. NG24: N'wark T 3F 35
Chestnut Cl. LN2: Scot 1H 13
   LN4: Meth 3H 29
Chestnut Copse NG24: New B 2F 37
Chestnut Cres. LN5: Bass 2D 30
Chestnut Dr. NG24: Scot 1H 13
Chestnut Gro. LN5: Wad 6C 22
Chestnut Rd. LN6: N Hyk 5K 21
Chestnuts, The LN2: Nett 1B 12
Chestnut St. LN1: Lin 1B 38 (1E 16)
Cheviot Cl. LN6: N Hyk 7J 21
Cheviot St. LN2: Lin 4E 38 (3G 17)
Chichester Rd. LN4: Brac B 3G 23
Chieftain Way LN6: Lin 6C 16
Chiltern Rd. LN5: Lin 4D 22
Chiltern Way LN6: N Hyk 7J 21
Chippendale Cl. LN6: Lin 1H 21
Chippendale Rd. LN6: Lin 1H 21
Chivenor Cl. LN6: Lin 5F 15
Christopher Cres. NG24: New B 4G 37
Christ's Hospital Ter.
   LN2: Lin 3C 38 (2F 17)
Church Ct. LN2: Scot 1G 13
Church Dr. LN6: Lin 5D 16
Church Hill LN4: Wash 4D 18
Churchill Av. LN4: Brac B 3F 23
Churchill Dr. NG24: N'wark T 3C 36
Church La. LN1: Sax .1D 8
   LN2: Lin 1C 38 (1F 17)
   LN2: Scot 1G 13
   LN3: C Will 1G 19
   LN3: Ree 5H 13
   LN4: Meth 5J 29
   LN4: Pott 2A 28
   LN5: Carl M 7C 30
   LN5: Harm 7E 26
   LN5: Nav 4H 31
   LN5: Wad 3E 26
   NG23: Coll 3H 33
   NG23: N Mus, S Mus 7B 32
   NG24: Bald 5J 37
Church Rd. LN1: Sax 2E 8
   LN4: Bran 4E 24
   LN6: Skel 2E 14
Church Row NG23: N Mus 4C 32
   LN2: Scot 7G 5

Church St. LN5: Carl M 7C **30**
  LN8: Wrag 3G **7**
  NG23: Coll 5G **33**
  NG24: N'wark T 7D **34**
Church Vw. LN2: Nett 2B **12**
  NG24: Bald 5H **37**
Church Vw. Cres. LN3: Fis 3K **19**
Church Wlk. LN4: Meth 5H **29**
  (not continuous)
  LN5: Harm 7E **26**
  NG24: N'wark T 7D **34**
Cirencester Cl. LN6: N Hyk 7H **21**
City Crematorium, The LN4: Lin 5H **17**
City Sports Cen. 7A **16**
City Sq. Cen. LN5: Lin 5C **38** (3F **17**)
Clara Ter. LN1: Lin 3B **38** (2E **16**)
Clare Cl. LN5: Lin 4D **22**
Claremont St. LN2: Lin 3G **17**
Clarence Ho. LN2: Lin 6G **11**
Clarence St. LN1: Lin 7E **10**
Clarendon Ct. LN4: Wash 5D **18**
Clarendon Gdns. LN1: Lin 5E **10**
Clarendon Vw. LN1: Lin 5E **10**
Claricoates Dr. NG24: Codd 5J **35**
Clarina St. LN2: Lin 3H **17**
Clark Cres. LN2: Lin 6J **11**
Clarke Av. LN4: H'ton 7G **19**
  NG24: N'wark T 3C **36**
Clarke Rd. LN6: Lin 3J **21**
  LN6: N Hyk 7J **21**
Clarks La. NG24: N'wark T 5F **35**
Clasketgate LN2: Lin 4C **38** (3F **17**)
Claudius Rd. LN6: N Hyk 7H **21**
Clay La. LN5: Bass 4A **30**
  LN5: Carl M 7A **30**
  LN6: T Hill 7A **20**
  NG24: N'wark T 1F **37**
Clayton Cl. NG24: N'wark T 2E **36**
Clayton Ho. LN6: Lin 3D **16**
  (off The Pavilions Student Village)
Clayton Rd. LN5: Lin 1D **22**
Clematis App. LN6: Lin 6G **15**
Clematis Cl. LN4: Bran 3D **24**
Clement Av. NG24: Bald 5J **37**
Clement Cl. LN4: Bran 4F **25**
Cleveland Av. LN6: N Hyk 7H **21**
Cleveland Sq. NG24: N'wark T 2D **36**
Cliff Av. LN2: Nett 2A **12**
Cliffe Ct. LN2: Welt 2C **4**
Cliff La. LN4: Wash 6D **18**
Cliff Nook La. NG24: N'wark T 6E **34**
Cliff Rd. LN2: Welt 2B **4**
  LN5: Well 7G **31**
Cliffside LN5: Well 6J **31**
Clifton Cres. NG24: N'wark T 4G **35**
Clifton Ho. NG24: N'wark T 4D **36**
Clifton St. LN5: Lin 7D **38** (4G **17**)
Clint La. LN5: Nav 4J **31**
Clinton Arms Ct. NG24: N'wark T 7D **34**
  (off St Mark's Pl.)
Clinton St. NG24: N'wark T 7D **34**
Clipsham Cl. NG24: Bald 3J **37**
Clive Av. LN6: Lin 6C **16**
Cloisters, The LN2: Lin 2E **38**
  LN2: Welt 1B **4**
Close, The LN3: Fis 1K **19**
  LN4: Brac B 4G **23**
  NG24: N'wark T 7E **34**
Clover Rd. LN4: Brac B 5G **23**
Club Ct. NG24: Bald 4H **37**
Cludd Av. NG24: N'wark T 7J **35**
Clumber Av. NG24: N'wark T 2E **36**
Clumber St. LN5: Lin 7E **16**
Coalport Cl. LN6: Lin 7H **15**
Cockburn Way LN5: Harm 7E **26**
CODDINGTON 6K **35**
Coddington Rd. NG24: Bald 4K **37**
Coging Cl. NG24: New B 5G **37**
Colchester M. LN6: N Hyk 7H **21**
Coleby St. LN2: Lin 3H **17**
Colegrave St. LN5: Lin 7E **16**
Coleman Av. NG24: New B 4F **37**
Colenso Ter. LN1: Lin 2D **16**
Coleraine Cl. LN5: Lin 5D **22**
Coleridge Gdns. LN2: Lin 6J **11**
Coleridge Grn. LN2: Lin 6J **11**
Coleridge Rd. NG24: Bald 3J **37**

Collection, The:
  Art & Archaeology in Lincolnshire
  ....3C **38**
College Cl. LN1: Lin 7F **11**
COLLINGHAM 4G **33**
Collingham Station (Rail) 4J **33**
Collingwood LN6: N Hyk 7J **21**
Collinson La. NG24: Bald 7J **37**
Collis Cl. NG24: N'wark T 7H **35**
Colne Cl. LN6: Lin 4K **21**
Coningsby Cres. LN4: Brac B 2F **23**
Coningsby St. LN2: Lin 5E **38** (3G **17**)
Coniston Dr. LN6: N Hyk 5A **22**
Connaught Ter. LN5: Lin 2D **22**
Constable Av. LN6: Lin 2A **22**
Constable Cl. LN6: Lin 2A **22**
Constance Av. LN6: Lin 3J **21**
Conway Dr. LN6: N Hyk 5B **22**
Coopers Cl. LN2: Nett 1B **12**
Coopers Holt Cl. LN6: Skel 3E **14**
Coopers Yd. NG24: N'wark T 7C **34**
Cordage Cl. LN1: Lin 3B **38** (2E **16**)
Cormack La. NG24: Bald 7K **37**
Corn Cl. LN3: Fis 3K **19**
Cornflower Way LN6: N Hyk 7F **21**
Cornhill LN5: Lin 5C **38** (3F **17**)
Cornhill Mkt. LN5: Lin 5C **38**
Cornus Cl. LN4: Bran 3E **24**
Cornwall Ho. LN2: Lin 6G **11**
Cornwallis Rd. LN3: Lin 3K **17**
Cornwood Cl. LN2: Lin 6B **12**
Coronation St. NG24: New B 3G **37**
Corporation St. LN1: Lin 4C **38** (3E **16**)
  LN2: Lin 4C **38** (3F **17**)
Correen Cl. LN5: Lin 5D **22**
Cosford Cl. LN6: Lin 6F **15**
Cosgrove Cl. LN6: Lin 1A **22**
Cotham La. NG24: Hawt 6B **36**
Cotman Rd. LN6: Lin 1A **22**
Cotman Wlk. LN6: Lin 1A **22**
Cotswold Cl. LN6: N Hyk 7J **21**
Cottage Cl. NG24: Bald 6H **37**
Cottage La. LN6: Lin 3B **22**
  NG23: Coll 7G **33**
Cottage Paddock, The LN6: Lin 2B **22**
Cottesford Pl. LN2: Lin 1C **38** (1F **17**)
Cottesmore Rd. LN6: Lin 1G **21**
Cottingham Ct. LN2: Dunh 2E **4**
Cottingham Dr. LN2: Lin 7H **11**
Cotton Smith Way LN2: Nett 1B **12**
Coulson Rd. LN6: Lin 5D **16**
Coult Av. LN6: N Hyk 7J **21**
Coupland Cl. LN5: Wad 4F **27**
Court 2 LN6: Lin 3C **16**
Court 3 LN6: Lin 3D **16**
Court 4 LN6: Lin 3D **16**
Court 13 LN6: Lin 3D **16**
Court 14 LN6: Lin 3D **16**
Court 15 LN6: Lin 3D **16**
Court 16 LN6: Lin 3D **16**
Court 17 LN6: Lin 3D **16**
Courtfield Cl. LN2: Scot 1H **13**
Cow La. NG24: N'wark T 6D **34**
Cowpaddle La. LN4: Wash 4J **19**
Cowper Dr. LN2: Lin 6J **11**
Crab La. NG23: N Mus 5C **32**
Cranbourne Chase LN6: N Hyk 7H **21**
Cranbourn M. LN4: Wash 5F **19**
Crane Gro. LN6: Lin 7C **16**
Crankley La. NG23: N'wark T 3B **34**
Cranmer Rd. NG24: N'wark T 3D **36**
Cranwell Cl. NG24: N'wark T 6H **35**
Cranwell St. LN5: Lin 5E **16**
Craven St. LN5: Lin 6D **16**
Craypool La. LN2: Scot 7H **5**
Crees La. NG24: N'wark T 2A **36**
Crescent, The LN2: Nett 1B **12**
  LN3: Fis 3K **19**
  LN4: Brac B 4G **23**
  LN8: Wrag 4H **7**
  NG24: N'wark T 2E **36**
Crescent Cl. LN2: Nett 1C **12**
Crescent M. LN5: Harm 7E **26**
Cresta Cl. LN6: N Hyk 6H **21**
Crew Rd. NG23: Coll 3J **33**
Croft, The LN2: Nett 2C **12**
  NG24: N'wark T 7E **34**

Croft La. LN3: C Will 6G **13**
  LN5: Bass 2D **30**
Crofton Cl. LN3: Lin 2K **17**
Crofton Dr. LN3: Lin 2K **17**
Crofton Rd. LN3: Lin 2K **17**
Croft St. LN2: Lin 4D **38** (3G **17**)
Cromer Cl. LN6: N Hyk 6A **22**
Cromwell Cl. LN4: Wash 4C **18**
Cromwell Rd. NG24: N'wark T 1F **37**
Cromwell St. LN2: Lin 3H **17**
Crossfield Rd. LN5: Nav 5J **31**
Cross La. LN6: N Hyk 7K **21**
  NG23: Coll 3J **33**
  NG24: Bald 7G **37**
Cross o'Cliff Cl. LN5: Lin 1E **22**
Cross o'Cliff Hill LN5: Brac B, Lin ...7E **16**
Cross Spencer St. LN5: Lin 6E **16**
Cross St. LN2: Nett 2B **12**
  LN4: Pott 2A **28**
  LN5: Lin 7C **38** (5F **17**)
  NG24: N'wark T 7E **34**
Crowland Dr. LN6: Lin 7K **15**
Crow La. NG23: S Mus 6A **32**
Crown Cl. NG23: Coll 3H **33**
Crown Mill Cott. LN5: Lin 5E **16**
Crown St. NG24: N'wark T 1D **36**
Crow Pk. LN6: S Hyk 7E **20**
Croxton Dr. LN6: Lin 1K **21**
Crusader Rd. LN6: Lin 5C **16**
Cullen Cl. NG24: N'wark T 6C **34**
Cullin Cl. LN5: Lin 5D **22**
Cumberland Av. LN5: Well 6H **31**
Cumberland Gap LN5: Well 6H **31**
Curle Av. LN2: Lin 1G **17**
Currie Rd. NG24: N'wark T 5E **34**
Curtis Cl. NG23: Coll 3H **33**
Curtis Dr. LN4: H'ton 6F **19**
Curtois Cl. LN4: Bran 4E **24**
Curzon M. LN4: Wash 5F **19**
Cydonia App. LN6: Lin 6G **15**

D

D'Aincourt Pk. LN4: Bran 3C **24**
Dalderby Cres. LN2: Nett 2A **12**
Dale Av. LN3: C Will 7G **13**
Dale Cres. LN4: Bald 6J **37**
Dales, The LN2: Nett 2B **12**
Dale St. LN5: Lin 4H **17**
Dale Vw. Est. LN6: N Hyk 5A **22**
Daleview Mdws. LN6: N Hyk 6A **22**
Dale Way NG24: Bald 6K **37**
Dalewood LN5: Lin 5D **22**
Dane Cl. LN4: Meth 5G **29**
Danes Cotts. LN2: Lin 3C **38**
Danes Courtyard LN2: Lin 3C **38**
Danesgate LN2: Lin 3C **38** (2F **17**)
Danes Ter. LN2: Lin 3C **38** (2F **17**)
  (not continuous)
Daniel Cres. LN4: H'ton 5F **19**
Daniel Gdns. LN4: H'ton 6F **19**
Dankerwood Rd. LN6: S Hyk 7E **20**
Daphne Cl. LN4: Bran 3E **24**
Dart Av. LN6: N Hyk 5A **22**
Darwin Cl. LN5: Wad 1D **26**
Darwin Ct. LN2: Lin 1H **17**
Daubeney Av. LN1: Sax 3F **9**
David Av. LN1: Lin 5D **10**
David Lloyd Leisure
  Lincoln 6H **9**
Davy's La. LN4: Brac B 4G **23**
Dawson Cl. LN6: Lin 1K **21**
Dawsons La. LN3: Ree 5H **13**
Deacon Rd. LN2: Lin 1J **17**
Deane Cl. NG23: Coll 3H **33**
Deane Wlk. LN2: Dunh 3D **4**
Dean Rd. LN2: Lin 1J **17**
Deansway LN4: Bran 2C **24**
De Caldwell Dr. NG24: N'wark T ...2C **36**
Deepdale La. LN2: Nett 1A **12**
Dees, The LN6: Dodd 6C **14**
De Havilland Way
  NG24: N'wark T 2A **36**
Dellfield Av. LN6: Lin 5G **15**
Dellfield Cl. LN6: Lin 4G **15**
Dellfield Ct. LN6: Lin 5G **15**

Deloraine Ct. LN2: Lin 2C 38 (2F 17)
LN4: Wash 4D 18
Delph Rd. LN6: N Hyk 7K 21
Denbigh Ct. NG23: Coll 3H 33
Denby Dale Cl. LN6: Lin 4G 15
Dene, The LN2: Nett 1B 12
LN6: Skel 3F 15
Dene Cl. LN6: Skel 3F 15
Denefield LN6: Skel 3F 15
Dene Rd. LN6: Skel 3F 15
Dennis Brown Ct. LN1: Sax 3F 9
Denton Cl. NG24: Bald 5G 37
Denton Ho. LN6: Lin 6K 15
Denzlingen Cl. LN6: N Hyk 6H 21
Depot St. LN1: Lin 4A 38 (3D 16)
Depot Yd. NG24: N'wark T 6D 34
(off Slaughter Ho. La.)
Derby St. LN5: Lin 6E 16
Derek Miller Ct. LN1: Lin 4A 38 (3E 16)
Derwent Cl. LN6: Lin 5A 22
Derwent Ct. NG24: Bald 5H 37
Derwent St. LN1: Lin 2C 16
Derwent Way NG24: N'wark T 5F 35
Devon Farm Cl. NG24: N'wark T . . .1B 36
Devon Rd. NG24: N'wark T 2C 36
Devon St. LN2: Lin 3J 17
De Wint Av. LN6: Lin 2A 22
De Wint Cl. LN4: Meth 4H 29
LN6: Lin 2B 22
De Wint Ct. LN6: Lin 2B 22
De Wint Pl. LN6: Lin 2B 22
Dickinson Way NG23: N Mus 3C 32
Digby Cl. LN6: Lin 7G 15
Dixon Cl. LN6: Lin 5D 16
Dixon Ct. LN6: Lin 5D 16
Dixon St. LN5: Lin 5C 16
LN6: Lin 5C 16
Dixon Way LN6: Lin 5D 16
Dixon Way Trad. Est.
LN6: Lin 6D 16
Dobsons Quay NG24: N'wark T . . .6D 34
DODDINGTON PARK 1G 21
DODDINGTON 5A 14
Doddington Av. LN6: Lin 3A 22
Doddington Hall & Gdns. 5A 14
Doddington Rd. LN6: Lin 1F 21
LN6: Whi 2A 20
Doddington Rdbt. LN6: Lin 1E 20
Doe Cl. LN6: With S 6A 26
Doncaster Gdns. LN5: Nav 5J 31
Dorchester Way LN6: N Hyk 7H 21
Dore Av. LN6: N Hyk 5J 21
Dorewood Ct. NG24: Bald 4J 37
Dorner Av. NG24: N'wark T 1B 36
Dorothy Av. LN4: Brac B 4G 23
Dorrigan Cl. LN1: Lin 6C 10
Dorset St. LN2: Lin 3J 17
Doughty's Ct. LN5: Lin 5D 38
Doulton Cl. LN6: Lin 7H 15
Dovecote Dr. LN2: Welt 1E 4
Dove Dale LN6: N Hyk 5K 21
Dowding M. LN3: Lin 3A 18
Dowding Rd. LN3: Lin 2A 18
Drake Av. LN4: Wash 5D 18
Drake St. LN1: Lin 2C 16
Drill Hall 4C 38
DRINSEY NOOK 5A 8
Drinsey Nook La. NG23: Thor 7A 8
Drive, The NG24: Wint 1G 35
Drove, The LN6: S Hyk 7F 21
Drove La. NG24: Codd 1J 35
(not continuous)
Drury La. LN1: Lin 3B 38 (2E 16)
Drury St. LN4: Meth 5J 29
Dryden Av. LN2: Lin 7H 11
NG24: Bald 3J 37
Dunford Rd. LN5: Lin 7D 38 (4F 17)
DUNHOLME 3E 4
Dunholme Av. NG24: N'wark T 1D 36
Dunholme Cl. LN2: Welt 2D 4
Dunholme Cl. LN2: Lin 5G 11
Dunholme Rd. LN2: Scot 4F 5
LN2: Welt 1D 4
Dunkirk Rd. LN1: Lin 7D 10
Dunlop St. LN5: Lin 5F 17
Dunmore Cl. LN5: Lin 4D 22
DUNSTON 2G 29

Dunston Cl. LN2: Lin 5G 11
Dunston Fen La. LN4: Duns 1J 29
Dunston Heath La. LN4: Duns 2F 29
Dunston Rd. LN4: Duns, Meth 2H 29
Durham Cl. LN4: Brac B 3G 23
LN6: Lin 4H 15
Durham Cres. LN4: Wash 5F 19
Dykes End NG23: Coll 5H 33

E

Eagle Dr. LN2: Welt 1C 4
Eagle La. LN6: T Hill 7A 20
Eagle Rd. LN6: Whi 2A 20
Earls Dr. LN6: Lin 6D 16
Earlsfield LN4: Bran 3F 25
Earlsfield Cl. LN4: Bran 2F 21
Earp Av. NG24: N'wark T 1E 36
East Av. LN4: Brac B 4G 23
East Bight LN2: Lin 1C 38 (1F 17)
(not continuous)
Eastbourne St. LN2: Lin 3G 17
Eastbrook Rd. LN6: Lin 3A 22
Eastcliff Rd. LN2: Lin 2G 17
East Cft. LN3: C Will 6G 13
(not continuous)
Eastcroft LN1: Sax 1E 8
Eastern Ct. NG24: N'wark T 7E 34
Eastern Ter. LN5: Lin 5D 16
Eastern Ter. La. NG24: N'wark T . . .7E 34
East Fld. LN5: Bass 3E 30
Eastfield NG23: N Mus 4C 32
Eastfield Cl. LN2: Welt 1E 4
Eastfield La. LN2: Welt 1D 4
Eastfield St. LN2: Lin 3H 17
Eastgate LN2: Lin 2C 38 (2F 17)
LN5: Bass 3D 30
Eastgate Cl. LN2: Lin 2E 38 (2G 17)
Eastholm LN2: Lin 6B 12
Eastleigh Cl. LN6: Lin 5F 15
East Liberty LN2: Lin 2J 17
E. Mill Ga. LN3: C Will 7G 13
Eastoft Ho. LN6: Lin 6K 15
East St. LN2: Nett 1B 12
Eastway LN2: Nett 2C 12
Ebony Gro. LN6: Lin 5G 15
Eccleston's Yd. NG24: N'wark T 7D 34
(off Market Pl.)
Eddystone Dr. LN6: N Hyk 6A 22
Edendale Gdns. LN1: Lin 5E 10
Edendale Vw. LN1: Lin 5E 10
Edge Cl. NG23: N Mus 2C 32
Edgehill LN5: Lin 5D 22
Edgehill Dr. NG24: N'wark T 7J 35
Edinburgh Ho. LN2: Lin 6G 11
Edinburgh Sq. LN5: Wad 2G 27
Edlington Cl. LN2: Lin 5F 11
Edna St. LN5: Lin 5F 17
Edward Av. NG24: N'wark T 7C 34
Edward Barker Rd. LN4: H'ton 7G 19
Edward Jermyn Dr. NG24: N'wark T . .3F 35
Edward St. LN6: Lin 6D 16
Egerton Rd. LN2: Lin 1H 17
Egret Gro. LN6: Lin 6H 15
Elder Cl. LN6: With S 6A 26
Elder St. LN5: Lin 2D 22
Eldon St. NG24: N'wark T 1D 36
Eleanor Cl. LN5: Lin 7E 16
Elevation Ct. LN2: Lin 3J 17
Elizabeth Av. LN6: N Hyk 6K 21
Elizabeth Rd. NG24: N'wark T 3C 36
Elk Racing Outdoor Karting Circuit 1K 35
Ellerslie Cl. NG24: N'wark T 6E 34
Ellesmere Av. LN2: Lin 2K 17
Elliott Rd. LN5: Lin 7E 38 (5G 17)
Ellis Mill 1A 38
Ellison Cl. LN2: Scot 1H 13
Ellison Ho. LN6: Lin 3D 16
(off The Pavilions Student Village)
Ellison St. LN5: Lin 2D 22
Elm Av. LN3: C Will 1F 19
NG24: N'wark T 2F 37
Elm Cl. LN1: Sax 2F 9
LN6: N Hyk 5K 21
NG24: Bald 2F 37
Elmdene LN2: Scot 7H 5

Elm Dr. LN2: Scot 1H 13
Elmwood Cl. LN6: Lin 5H 15
Elsham Cl. LN6: Lin 6H 15
Elsham Cres. LN6: Lin 6H 15
Elton Cl. LN1: Lin 6C 10
NG24: Bald 5H 37
Elvin Cl. LN2: Lin 7F 11
Elvington Cl. LN6: Lin 1F 21
Elvington Rd. LN6: Lin 1F 21
Ely Cl. LN4: Brac B 3G 23
Ely St. LN1: Lin 2D 16
Emmendingen Av. NG24: N'wark T . .4F 35
Enderby Cl. LN4: Wash 4C 18
Ennerdale Cl. LN6: Lin 5H 15
Enright Cl. NG24: N'wark T 2D 36
Enterprise Pk. NG24: N'wark T 4G 35
Epsom Cl. LN6: Lin 6F 15
Epsom Rd. LN6: Lin 6F 15
Epworth Vw. LN1: Lin 5E 10
ERMINE .5G 11
Ermine Cl. LN1: Lin 5E 10
Ermine Dr. LN5: Nav 4K 31
Ernest Ter. LN1: Lin 1C 38 (1F 17)
Escombe Vw. LN1: Lin 5D 10
Eshings, The LN2: Welt 1D 4
Esk Cl. LN6: Lin 3K 21
Estwaite Cl. LN6: N Hyk 5A 22
Eton Av. NG24: N'wark T 2C 36
Eton Cl. LN6: Lin 3H 15
NG24: N'wark T 2D 36
Eton Rd. LN4: Wash 5E 18
Euston Cl. LN6: Lin 4H 15
Eve Gdns. LN4: Wash 5F 19
Everest Ct. NG24: Bald 4J 37
Ewart St. LN1: Lin 1D 22
Exchange Arc. LN5: Lin 5C 38
Exchange Cl. LN6: N Hyk 3J 21
Exchange Rd. LN6: Lin 3J 21
Exchequer Gate 2C 38 (2F 17)
Exchequer Ga. LN2: Lin 2C 38 (2F 17)
Exeter Cl. LN4: Wash 5G 19
Exley Sq. LN2: Lin 7K 11
Exmoor Cl. LN6: N Hyk 6H 21
Eyam Way LN6: N Hyk 6K 21

F

Fairfax Av. NG24: N'wark T 3C 36
Fairfax St. LN5: Lin 1D 22
Fairfield Av. NG24: New B 3H 37
Fairfield St. LN2: Lin 3H 17
Fairleas LN4: Bran 3F 25
Fairway NG24: N'wark T 3B 36
Falcon Vw. LN6: Lin 6H 15
Faldingworth Cl. LN6: Lin 7G 15
Falklands Cl. LN1: Lin 5E 10
Falstone Av. NG24: N'wark T 2F 37
Far End LN5: Booth G 1H 31
Far La. LN5: Wad 3E 26
Farmers Wlk. NG24: N'wark T 3G 35
Farm Vw. LN2: Welt 1D 4
Farndon La. NG24: Hawt 6A 36
Farndon Rd. NG24: N'wark T 2A 36
Farrar Cl. NG24: N'wark T 5G 35
Farrier Ct. LN4: Meth 4H 29
Farrier Rd. LN6: Lin 2F 21
Farrington Cl. LN6: Lin 4H 15
Farrington Cres. LN6: Lin 4H 15
Far Wharf LN1: Lin 4A 38 (3D 16)
Favell Rd. LN4: Wash 4D 18
Fawsley Cl. LN2: Lin 6A 12
Fayid La. LN4: Noct 5C 28
Featherby Pl. LN5: Lin 6E 16
Fen La. LN1: S Car 1A 10
LN5: Bass 1E 30
LN6: N Hyk 5A 22
NG24: Bald, Barn W 4K 37
Fen Rd. LN1: Bur . . . . .6J 9 & 4A 10
LN4: H'ton, Wash 7H 19
LN4: Meth 4H 29
LN4: Wash 4F 19
Fenton Cl. NG24: N'wark T 5F 35
Fenton Pl. LN2: Lin 3G 17
Fen Vw. LN4: H'ton 7H 19
Ferguson Ho. LN5: Lin 5J 15
Fern Cl. LN6: Lin 3A 22

Fern Gro. LN3: C Will 1F 19
Fernleigh Av. LN4: Brac B 5G 23
FERNWOOD 6J 37
Ferry La. LN4: Wash 4D 18
   LN6: Skel .1F 15
   NG23: N Mus 4C 32
Ferry Rd. LN3: Fis 3K 19
Ferryside LN3: Fis 3K 19
Ferryside Gdns. LN3: Fis 4K 19
Field Cl. LN2: Nett 2C 12
   LN2: Welt 1C 4
Field Farm La. LN4: Meth 4J 29
Filey Cl. LN6: N Hyk 4A 22
Finch Cl. LN6: Lin 6J 15
Finch Way LN8: Wrag 4G 7
Finningley Cl. LN6: Lin 1H 21
Finningley Rd. LN6: Lin 2H 21
Firth Rd. LN5: Lin 7A 38 (4D 16)
   (not continuous)
   LN6: Lin 7A 38 (4D 16)
   (not continuous)
Fir Tree Av. LN5: Wad 7C 22
Firtree Av. LN6: Lin 5G 15
Fir Tree Cl. LN2: Scot 1G 13
Fisher Cl. NG23: Coll 3J 33
FISKERTON 1K 19
Fiskerton Dr. LN2: Lin 5F 11
Fiskerton Rd. LN3: C Will, Lin 2D 18
   LN3: Ree .5J 13
Fiskerton Rd. E. LN3: C Will 2G 19
Fitness First
   Lincoln 5D 16
Five Bells Jetty LN5: Bass 2D 30
Five Mile La. LN4: Wash 5K 19
Flaxengate LN2: Lin 4C 38 (3F 17)
Flaxley Rd. LN2: Lin 7A 12
Fleet St. LN1: Lin 2C 16
Fleming Dr. NG24: N'wark T 3F 35
Fleming Ho. LN5: Lin 2D 22
Flinders Cl. LN4: Meth 4G 29
Flinders Way LN3: C Will 7D 12
Flintham Cl. LN4: Meth 4G 29
Florence St. LN2: Lin 3H 17
Folkingham Cl. LN6: Lin 6H 15
Folly La. LN4: Bran 4A 24
Fontwell Cres. LN6: Lin 2A 22
Fordham Dr. LN6: Lin 6C 10
Fordham Ho. LN6: Lin 2B 22
Forge Cl. NG23: S Mus 7A 32
Forge Cotts. NG23: S Mus 7B 32
Forster Av. NG24: N'wark T 4C 36
Forsythia Cl. LN4: Bran 3D 24
Forum, The LN6: N Hyk 4K 21
Foss Bank LN1: Lin 3D 16
Fossdyke Gdns. LN1: Sax 3F 9
Fossdyke Ho. LN1: Sax 2B 8
Fosse Ct. LN4: Brac B 5G 23
Fosse Dr. LN6: N Hyk 4K 21
Fosse Gro. LN1: Sax 3F 9
Fosse Ho. LN6: Lin 2C 22
Fosse La. LN6: T Hill 7B 20
Fosse Rd. NG24: Farn 3A 36
   NG24: N'wark T 3A 36
Foss St. LN1: Lin 3D 16
Foster Lodge LN6: Lin 3D 16
   (off The Pavilions Student Village)
Foster Rd. NG23: Coll 3H 33
Fosters Cl. LN5: Nav 4J 31
Foster's Gdns. LN4: Pott 1B 28
Foster St. LN5: Lin 7A 38 (5E 16)
Foston Cres. LN4: Lin 7K 15
Foundry Cl. NG24: N'wark T 5D 34
Fountain Ct. LN5: Lin 2D 22
Fox Covert LN2: Scot 1J 13
   LN6: S Hyk 6E 20
Fox Covert La. LN2: Dunh 1J 5
Foxfield Cl. LN6: Skel 1E 14
Foxglove Cl. NG24: New B 4G 37
Foxglove Way LN5: Lin 4D 22
Fox Hollow LN6: With S 6B 26
Foyle Cl. LN5: Lin 6D 38
Francis Hill Ct. LN2: Lin 1D 38 (1F 17)
Francis St. LN1: Lin 1F 17
Franklin Cl. LN4: Meth 4H 29
Franklin Way LN3: C Will 7D 12
Frank St. LN5: Lin 5E 16

Frank Swaby Ct. LN5: Lin 1E 22
Frank Wright Ct. LN2: Lin 6J 11
Frederick St. LN2: Lin 3J 17
Freeman Rd. LN6: N Hyk 4H 21
Freeschool La. LN2: Lin 5C 38 (3F 17)
Freslon Ct. LN2: Welt 1B 4
Friars Cres. NG24: N'wark T 3D 36
Friars La. LN2: Lin 4D 38 (3F 17)
Friars M. LN2: Lin 4D 38
Friary Gdns. NG24: N'wark T 6E 34
Friary M. NG24: N'wark T 6E 34
Friary Rd. NG24: N'wark T 7E 34
Friary Vs. NG24: N'wark T 6E 34
Frome Cl. LN6: Lin 2H 21
Front St. LN4: Duns 2G 29
Fulbeck Ho. LN6: Lin 1B 22
Fulford Pl. LN2: Lin 1J 17
Fulmar Ct. LN6: Lin 7J 15
Fulmar Rd. LN6: Lin 6H 15
   (not continuous)
Fulmen Cl. LN1: Lin 7C 10
Fulstow Rd. LN2: Lin 5H 11
Furndown Ct. LN6: Lin 7F 15
Furrow Cl. LN2: Welt 3C 4

G

Gabriel Cres. LN2: Lin 7A 12
Gage Ct. LN2: Lin 7K 11
   (off Stark Way)
Gail Gro. LN4: H'ton 6E 18
Gainsborough Dr. NG24: N'wark T 4F 35
Gainsborough Gdns. LN6: Lin 1B 22
Gainsborough Rd. LN1: D Noo, Sax 4A 8
   NG24: Wint 2G 35
Gaitskell Way NG24: Bald 4J 37
Gala Bingo
   Lincoln 5C 38
Gamage Cl. NG24: Bald 5J 37
Garden Ct. LN1: Lin 1C 16
Gardenfield LN6: Skel 4F 15
Gardiner Av. NG24: Bald 6K 37
Garfield Cl. LN1: Lin 5D 10
Garfield Vw. LN1: Lin 5D 10
Garmston St. LN2: Lin 3C 38 (2F 17)
Garratt Cl. LN4: H'ton 7F 19
Garrick Cl. LN5: Lin 4D 22
Garside Vw. LN2: Lin 2K 17
Gas La. LN5: Nav 4J 31
Gateway, The NG24: N'wark T 7F 35
Gateway Ct. LN6: S Hyk 7F 21
Gaunt St. LN5: Lin 7A 38 (4E 16)
Gayton Ct. LN2: Lin 6G 11
Geneva Av. LN2: Lin 7H 11
George's M. LN1: Sax 2D 8
George St. LN5: Lin 4H 17
   NG24: N'wark T 6E 34
Gerald's Cl. LN2: Lin 1H 17
Gerrard M. LN4: Wash 5F 19
Gibbeson St. LN5: Lin 6E 16
Gibraltar Hill LN1: Lin 3B 38 (2E 16)
Gibson Cl. LN4: Bran 3E 24
Gibson Cres. NG24: New B 5G 37
Gibson Grn. LN6: With S 5C 26
Gibson Ho. LN2: Lin 5G 11
Gilbert Way NG24: Bald 6K 37
Gildesburgh Rd. LN4: Wash 5D 18
Gill Ho. NG24: N'wark T 4E 36
Gilmores La. NG24: Bald 7K 37
Gilstrap Cen., The 6D 34
Gilstrap Cl. NG24: N'wark T 7H 35
Gladstone Rd. NG24: N'wark T 2D 36
Gleanings, The LN5: Nav 4K 31
Glebe End LN4: Can 6H 17
Glebelands NG23: N Mus 5C 32
Glebe Pk. NG24: New B 2G 37
Gleedale LN6: N Hyk 5J 21
Glenarm Cres. LN5: Lin 4D 22
Glenbank Cl. LN6: Lin 4K 21
Glendon Cl. LN5: Lin 4D 22
Gleneagles Gro. LN4: H'ton 5F 19
Glentham Cl. LN6: Lin 4B 22
Glenwood Gro. LN6: Lin 5D 16
Gloucester Cl. LN4: Brac B 3G 23
Gloucester Ho. LN2: Lin 6G 11
Glovers La. NG24: Bald 4H 37

Glynn Rd. LN1: Lin 5E 10
Glynn Vw. LN1: Lin 5E 10
Godber Dr. LN4: Brac B 4F 23
Goldcrest Cl. LN6: Lin 5J 15
Goldfinch Cl. LN6: Skel 3E 14
Goldsmith Rd. NG24: Bald 3H 37
Goldsmith Wlk. LN2: Lin 6J 11
Goldson Way NG23: N Mus 5C 32
Goldstraw La. NG24: Bald 6J 37
Good La. LN1: Lin 1F 17
Goodwin Cl. NG24: N'wark T 7H 35
Goodwin La. NG24: Bald 7K 37
Goodwood Way LN6: Lin 7G 15
Gopher Rd. NG24: N'wark T 3D 36
Gordon Rd. LN1: Lin 2C 38 (2F 17)
Gorehall Dr. LN2: Welt 1C 4
Gorse La. LN5: Carl M 5B 30
Gorse Rd. NG24: N'wark T 3D 36
Gothic Cl. LN6: Lin 7H 15
Goxhill Cl. LN6: Lin 7H 15
Goxhill Gro. LN6: Lin 7H 15
Grace Av. LN6: Lin, N Hyk 4G 21
Grace St. LN5: Lin 5F 17
Grafton St. LN2: Lin 3H 17
Graham Cl. NG24: New B 4F 37
Grainsby Cl. LN2: Lin 2C 22
Granary Cl. LN4: Meth 5G 29
   LN5: Wad 4F 27
Granby Av. NG24: N'wark T 2E 36
Granby Dr. NG24: Bald 5H 37
Granely Cl. LN2: Lin 7C 10
Grange, The NG23: N Mus 3C 32
Grange Cl. LN4: Can 6H 17
Grange Ct. LN5: Carl M 6C 30
Grange Cres. LN6: Lin 4B 22
Grange Dr. LN6: Lin 4A 22
Grange La. LN2: Ris 4F 11
   LN4: Can .6H 17
   LN4: H'ton 7F 19
   NG24: New B 7F 37
Grange Rd. LN4: Brac B 5F 23
   LN4: Meth 4J 29
   NG24: N'wark T 3B 36
Granson Way LN4: Wash 4C 18
Grantavon Ho. LN5: Lin 5B 38
Grantham Rd. LN4: Brac B 7F 23
   LN5: Booth G, Nav 1H 31
   LN5: Harm, Wad 1F 27
   LN5: Nav .5J 31
Granthams, The
   LN2: Dunh 3D 4
Grantham St. LN2: Lin 4C 38 (3F 17)
Grasmere Way LN6: Lin 5H 15
Grassmoor Cl. LN6: N Hyk 7H 21
Gravely Cl. LN6: Lin 1F 21
Grayson Grn. LN5: Well 7H 31
Gray St. LN1: Lin 1B 38 (1E 16)
   (not continuous)
Gt. Northern Ter. LN5: Lin 7D 38 (4G 17)
Gt. Northern Way LN5: Lin 4G 17
Great Nth. Rd. NG23: N Mus 3B 32
   NG23: N'wark T, N Mus, S Mus 7A 32
   NG24: Bald 7J 37
   NG24: N'wark T 5C 34
Greaves Cl. NG24: N'wark T 7H 35
Grebe Cl. LN6: N Hyk 6G 21
   NG24: New B 3G 37
Green, The LN2: Nett 2B 12
   LN2: Scot .7H 5
   LN3: Ree .5H 13
   LN4: Duns 2H 29
   LN4: Noct 6B 28
   LN4: Pott .2A 28
   LN5: Well .6H 31
   NG23: Coll 5G 33
Greenaway Cl. LN3: C Will 7G 13
Greenbank Dr. LN6: Lin 2A 22
Greenfield Cl. NG24: Codd 6J 35
Greenfields LN2: Nett 2C 12
Greenfinch Cres. LN6: With S 7A 26
Greenholme Cl. LN2: Lin 4G 11
Green La. LN1: Hard, Sax 4B 8
   LN2: Welt .3B 4
   LN3: C Will 1E 18
   LN4: Duns . . . . .6E 28 & 1K 29
   LN6: Lin .4D 16
   LN6: N Hyk 6K 21

Green La. LN6: Skel 1F **15**
  LN6: With S 6A **26**
  NG23: Coll 6J **33**
Green Man Rd. LN5: Nav 3J **31**
Greenock Way LN6: Lin 7F **15**
Greenway LN2: Scot 1H **13**
  LN2: Welt .1B **4**
  NG24: N'wark T 3C **36**
Greenwood Cl. LN5: Wad 7C **22**
Greestone Mt. LN2: Lin 3D **38** (2F **17**)
Greestone Pl. LN2: Lin 3D **38** (2F **17**)
Greestone Stairs LN2: Lin 3D **38**
Greestone Ter. LN2: Lin 3D **38** (2F **17**)
Greetwell Cl. LN2: Lin 2H **17**
Greetwell Ct. LN2: N Gre 5D **12**
Greetwell Ga. LN2: Lin 2E **38** (1G **17**)
Greetwell La. LN2: Lin 7B **12**
  LN2: Nett .2A **12**
  LN3: Lin 7B **12**
Greetwell Pl. LN2: Lin 1H **17**
                  (Greetwell Cl.)
  LN2: Lin 2J **17**
                  (Limekiln Way)
Greetwell Rd. LN2: Lin 2G **17**
  LN3: Lin 2G **17**
Gregg Hall Cl. LN6: Lin 3B **22**
Gregg Hall Cres. LN6: Lin 3B **22**
Gregg Hall Dr. LN6: Lin 3B **22**
Gresham Cl. NG24: N'wark T 7J **35**
Gresham St. LN1: Lin 2D **16**
Gresley Dr. LN6: Lin 5D **16**
Greyfriar's Pathway LN2: Lin 5C **38**
Greyling Cl. LN1: Lin 5E **10**
Greyling Vw. LN1: Lin 5E **10**
Griffin's La. LN5: Wad 1D **26**
Grinter Cl. LN6: N Hyk 7K **21**
Grosvenor Av. LN6: Lin 4H **15**
Grosvenor Ct. LN5: Lin 2D **22**
Grosvenor M. LN4: Wash 5F **19**
Grosvenor Rd. NG24: New B 4F **37**
Grosvenor Sq. LN5: Well 6H **31**
Grove, The LN2: Lin 1E **38** (1G **17**)
  LN2: Welt .2C **4**
Grove Cotts. NG24: N'wark T 1G **37**
Grove Sports Cen. 2G **37**
Grove St. NG24: New B 3F **37**
Groveview Rd. NG24: New B 3G **37**
Guildhall St. LN1: Lin 5B **38** (3E **16**)
  NG24: N'wark T 7E **34**
Gunby Av. LN6: Lin 1K **21**
Gynewell Gro. LN2: Lin 6J **11**

H

Habbanya Ri. LN4: Noct 5C **28**
Hackthorn Pl. LN2: Lin 5F **11**
Hackthorn Rd. LN2: Welt 1D **4**
Haddon Cl. LN6: Lin 5J **15**
Haddon Dr. NG24: Bald 5H **37**
Hadfield Rd. LN6: Lin 2A **22**
Hadleigh Dr. LN6: Lin 2K **21**
Hadrians Rd. LN4: Brac B 5G **23**
Haffenden Rd. LN2: Lin 7G **11**
Hainton Rd. LN6: Lin 2C **22**
Hale Cl. LN2: Lin 6A **12**
Hales La. LN5: Nav 4K **31**
Halfpenny Cl. LN2: Welt 1D **4**
Halfway Ho. Rdbt. LN6: Swin 5A **26**
HALFWAY HOUSES 5A **26**
Halifax Cl. LN6: Skel 2E **14**
Hallam Gro. LN6: Lin 7C **16**
Hall Dr. LN4: Can 6G **17**
  LN6: Lin 7D **16**
Hall Farm LN4: Can 6H **17**
Hallfield LN5: Bass 2C **30**
Hall Gdns. LN4: Can 6H **17**
Halliwell Cl. NG24: N'wark T 3F **35**
Hall La. LN2: Nett 1J **11**
  LN4: Bran .5B **24**
Halls Ct. LN4: Duns 1G **29**
Hall St. LN5: Well 6H **31**
Hallwath LN5: Bass 3C **30**
Hall Yd. LN4: Meth 5H **29**
Halton Cl. LN6: Lin 6F **15**
Hambleton Av. LN6: N Hyk 7H **21**
Hamilton Gro. LN6: Skel 3F **15**

Hamilton Rd. LN5: Lin 7E **16**
  LN6: N Hyk 5H **21**
Hampden Cl. LN6: Skel 2E **14**
Hampdens Cl. NG24: Codd 5J **35**
Hampden Way LN5: Wad 2G **27**
Hampton M. LN1: Lin 2D **16**
Hampton St. LN1: Lin 2A **38** (2D **16**)
Handley Ct. NG24: N'wark T 6D **34**
Hannah Cl. LN4: Bran 3E **24**
Hannah Cres. LN6: With S 5B **26**
Hannah Ho. LN2: Lin 5H **11**
Hanover Ho. LN2: Lin 5F **11**
Hansards Dr. LN8: Wrag 3G **7**
Harby Cl. LN6: Lin 4B **22**
  NG24: Bald 5H **37**
Harcourt St. NG24: N'wark T 1F **37**
Harding House Gallery 3C **38**
Hardings, The LN2: Welt 1D **4**
HARDWICK 1A **8**
Hardwick Av. NG24: N'wark T 1D **36**
Hardwick Pl. LN2: Lin 5G **11**
Harewood Av. NG24: N'wark T 1D **36**
Harewood Cres. LN6: N Hyk 5K **21**
Harewood Ho. LN2: Lin 5F **11**
Hargon La. NG24: Wint 1H **35**
Harlaxton Cl. LN6: Lin 1G **21**
Harlaxton Dr. LN6: Lin 1G **21**
HARMSTON 7E **26**
Harmston Pk. Av. LN5: Harm 7E **26**
Harpswell Rd. LN2: Lin 6G **11**
Harricot Cl. LN1: Lin 6C **10**
Harrier Ct. LN6: Lin 6H **15**
Harrington Av. LN6: Lin 6C **16**
Harrington Sq. LN4: H'ton 7G **19**
Harrison Pl. LN1: Lin 1B **38** (1E **16**)
Harris Rd. LN5: Wad 2F **27**
  LN6: Lin 1B **22**
Harrisson Pl. LN6: Lin 2H **21**
Harrow Cl. LN4: Wash 5E **18**
Harrows, The LN2: Welt 2C **4**
Hartland Av. LN6: N Hyk 6A **22**
Hartley St. LN2: Lin 3J **17**
HARTSHOLME .7K **15**
Hartsholme Country Pk. 7J **15**
Hartsholme Country Pk. Camp Site
  LN6: Lin 7K **15**
Hartsholme Country Pk. Vis. Cen. 6K **15**
Hartsholme Dr. LN6: Lin 6K **15**
Harvard Cl. LN4: Wash 5F **19**
Harvest Cl. LN4: Meth 5G **29**
Harvest Dr. NG24: N'wark T 3G **35**
Harvey St. LN1: Lin 3D **16**
Harwich Cl. LN5: Lin 4D **22**
Harwick Cl. LN1: Sax 2D **8**
Haslam Ho. NG24: N'wark T 4D **36**
Hatchet's La. NG24: N'wark T 4E **34**
Hatcliffe Gdns. LN2: Lin 5G **11**
Hathersage Av. LN6: N Hyk 5J **21**
Hatton Cl. LN6: Lin 7A **16**
Hatton Cl. NG23: N Mus 4C **32**
Hatton Gdns. NG24: N'wark T 1E **36**
Hawkshead Gro. LN2: Lin 5G **11**
Hawksmoor Cl. LN6: N Hyk 6H **21**
Hawthorn Av. LN3: C Will 7D **12**
  LN5: Wad .6C **22**
Hawthorn Chase LN2: Lin 6A **12**
Hawthorn Cl. LN4: Brac B 5G **23**
  LN4: H'ton .6G **19**
Hawthorn Rd. LN2: Lin 6A **12**
  LN3: C Will, Ree 6E **12**
Hawthorns, The LN2: Nett 1D **12**
Hawthorn Way LN5: Bass 2D **30**
HAWTON 5B **36**
Hawton La. NG24: New B 4E **36**
Hawton Rd. NG24: N'wark T 4B **36**
Haydor Av. LN2: Lin 5G **11**
Hayside Av. NG24: Bald 5F **37**
Hay Way LN8: Wrag 3G **7**
Hazel Cl. LN6: S Hyk 7E **20**
Hazel Gro. LN4: Meth 2B **4**
  NG24: New B 3G **37**
Hazel Ho. LN2: Lin 2J **17**
Hazelwood Av. LN6: Lin 5G **15**
Headland Way LN5: Nav 5J **31**
Healey Cl. NG23: Coll 4H **33**
Heath Cl. LN2: Welt 1B **4**

Heathcroft LN3: C Will 1G **19**
Heather Gdns. LN6: N Hyk 4J **21**
Heathfield Av. LN4: Bran 4F **25**
Heath La. LN2: Welt 2A **4**
  LN5: Booth G 1J **31**
Heathlea LN2: Scot 7G **5**
Heath Rd. LN2: Dunh 6B **4**
  LN2: Nett 1B **12**
  LN4: Brac B 5F **23**
  LN5: Nav 5J **31**
Heaton Cl. NG24: N'wark T 7H **35**
Hebden Moor Way LN6: N Hyk 7H **21**
Hedge La. LN6: With S 7H **26**
HEIGHINGTON 6G **19**
Heighington Fen LN4: Wash 5K **19**
Heighington Rd. LN4: Can 6H **17**
Helsby Rd. LN5: Lin 3D **22**
Hemplands, The NG23: Coll 3H **33**
Hemswell Av. LN6: Lin 1K **21**
Hendy Row LN5: Wad 2G **27**
Henley Cl. LN5: Lin 6D **16**
Henley St. LN5: Lin 6D **16**
Henley Way LN6: Lin 2H **21**
Henlow Cl. LN6: Lin 6F **15**
Henry St. LN5: Lin 5F **17**
Henson Dr. LN5: Nav 5J **31**
Henton Cl. NG24: Codd 5J **35**
Hercules Dr. NG24: N'wark T 1F **37**
Hereward St. LN1: Lin 1C **38** (1F **17**)
Heritage Ct. LN5: Nav 4J **31**
Hermit St. LN5: Lin 7B **38** (4E **16**)
Heron Vw. LN5: Lin 6J **15**
Heron Wlk. LN6: N Hyk 6G **21**
Heron Way NG24: New B 3G **37**
Herrington Av. LN2: Nett 1B **12**
Hewson Rd. LN1: Lin 2C **16**
Hewson's La. NG23: Coll 7H **33**
Heysham Cl. LN5: Lin 4D **22**
Hibaldstow Cl. LN6: Lin 7G **15**
Hibaldstow Rd. LN6: Lin 7G **15**
Hickory Rd. LN6: Lin 5G **15**
Higgins Cl. LN6: Lin 7J **15**
  NG24: N'wark T 5E **34**
Highcliffe LN5: Well 6H **31**
High Dike LN5: Booth G, Nav, Well 1K **31**
  LN5: Brac B, Wad 6H **27**
High Dyke LN5: Wad 1F **27**
Highfield Av. LN6: Lin 1B **22**
Highfield Rd. LN1: Sax 2E **8**
Highfields LN2: Nett 1C **12**
Highfields Ri. LN4: Meth 5G **29**
Highfield Ter. LN6: N Hyk 5A **22**
High Leas LN2: Nett 1C **12**
High Mdw. LN4: Wash 4E **18**
High Mdws. LN3: Fis 1K **19**
High St. LN1: Sax 2E **8**
  LN2: Lin 4C **38** (3F **17**)
  LN2: Nett 2B **12**
  LN3: C Will .1F **19**
  LN3: Fis 2K **19**
  LN3: Ree 5H **13**
  LN4: Bran .4E **24**
  LN4: H'ton .6F **19**
  LN4: Meth .4H **29**
  LN4: Wash 4D **18**
  LN5: Bass .3C **30**
  LN5: Carl M 6C **30**
  LN5: Harm .7E **26**
  LN5: Lin 7B **38** (6E **16**)
  LN5: Nav 4J **31**
  LN5: Wad .3F **27**
  LN5: Well 6H **31**
  LN6: Skel 1E **14**
  NG23: Coll .5G **33**
  NG23: Holm 4D **32**
Higson Rd. LN1: Lin 6D **10**
Hill, The LN6: Skel 2E **14**
Hillary Way NG24: Bald 4J **37**
Hillcroft LN4: Wash 4C **18**
Hillcroft Bus. Pk. LN6: Lin 2H **21**
Hillman Cl. LN4: Brac B 4F **23**
Hillside App. LN2: Lin 3J **17**
Hillside Av. LN2: Lin 3J **17**
Hillside Est. LN4: Bran 3E **24**
Hill Top LN5: Harm 7E **26**
Hill Vue Av. NG24: N'wark T 7F **35**
Hill Vue Gdns. NG24: N'wark T 7F **35**

Hinaidi La. LN4: Noct 5C 28
Hine Av. NG24: N'wark T 7H 35
Hobart Cl. LN5: Wad 1C 26
Hodson Cl. LN6: Skel 1F 15
Holdenby Cl. LN2: Lin 6A 12
Holdenby Rd. LN2: Lin 6A 12
Holden Cres. NG24: N'wark T 2D 36
Hollies Av. NG24: N'wark T 3F 35
Hollowdyke La. NG24: Bald 7K 37
　　　　　　　　　　　　　　(Great Nth. Rd.)
　　NG24: Bald 5K 37
　　　　　　　　　　　　　　　(Spring La.)
Holly Cl. LN3: C Will 1G 19
　　LN5: Lin .2D 22
Holly M. NG24: New B 3G 37
Holly St. LN5: Lin 2D 22
Hollywell Rd. LN5: Wad 6C 22
HOLME 3D 32
Holme Cl. LN6: T Hill 7C 20
Holme Dr. LN2: Scot 1G 13
Holme La. NG24: Wint 1G 35
Holmes, The LN1: Lin 5A 38 (3D 16)
Holmes Ct. LN5: Nav 4J 31
Holmes Field LN5: Bass 2D 30
Holmes La. LN2: Dunh 2E 4
Holmes Rd. LN1: Lin 4A 38 (3D 16)
Holmes Way LN8: Wrag 3F 7
Holmfield LN3: Fis . . . . .1K 19 & 3K 19
Holt, The NG24: N'wark T 2A 36
Holt Cl. LN6: N Hyk 7J 21
Holyrood Ho. LN2: Lin 5F 11
Home Cl. LN4: Brac B 4F 23
Home Ct. LN5: Well 6H 31
Honeyholes La. LN2: Dunh 4B 4
Honeypot Cl. LN2: Lin 6B 12
Honeys La. NG23: Thpe 7A 36
Honeysuckle Cl. LN5: Lin 5C 22
　　NG24: New B 3G 37
Honington App. LN1: Lin 6D 10
Honington Cres. LN1: Lin 6D 10
Hood St. LN5: Lin 5F 17
Hoop La. LN8: Lang W 7K 7
Hope St. LN5: Lin 5F 17
Horncastle La. LN2: Dunh 4A 4
Horncastle Rd. LN8: Wrag, Lang W . . .4H 7
Horner Cl. LN5: Lin 5C 22
Hornsby M. *LN6: Lin* *3D 16*
　　(off The Pavilions Student Village)
Horseshoe Cotts. NG23: Coll 4J 33
Hortonfield Dr. LN4: Wash 4E 18
Horton Pl. LN1: Sax 3G 9
Horton St. LN2: Lin 3H 17
Hospital Cotts. LN4: Brac B 3G 23
Hotchkin Av. LN1: Sax 3G 9
Hotel Rd. LN1: B Wat 7J 9
Hounsfield Cl. NG24: N'wark T 7J 35
Howard's Gdns. NG24: New B 4G 37
Howard St. LN1: Lin 2C 16
Howe Ct. LN2: Lin 7K 11
Howes Ct. NG24: N'wark T 7E 34
Huddlestones Wharf NG24: N'wark T . .7C 34
Hudson's La. LN4: H'ton 6G 19
Hughes Ford Way LN1: Sax 3F 9
Hughes Ho. LN6: Lin 2B 22
Hughson Wlk. LN2: Dunh 3E 4
Hundred Acres La. NG24: Bald 7G 37
Hungate LN1: Lin 4B 38 (3E 16)
　　　　　　　　　　　　　　(not continuous)
Hunters Cl. LN5: Wad 3F 27
Hunters Dr. LN4: Meth 4H 29
Hunt Lea Av. LN6: Lin 6C 16
Hurn Cl. LN6: Lin 6F 15
Hurstwood Cl. LN6: Lin 5K 11
Hutchinson Rd. NG24: N'wark T 7J 35
Hutson Dr. LN6: N Hyk 5K 21
Hyde Pk. Cl. LN6: N Hyk 4H 21
Hykeham Rd. LN6: Lin 4A 22
Hykeham Sailing Club 6F 21
Hykeham Station (Rail) 4H 21

I

Icknield Cl. LN4: Brac B 5G 23
Industrial Cotts. LN1: Lin 7C 10
Ingamells Dr. LN1: Sax 3G 9
Ingham Cl. LN6: Lin 4B 22

Ingleby Cres. LN2: Lin 5F 11
Inglewood Cl. NG24: Bald 6H 37
Inns Cl. LN6: N Hyk 4J 21
Ireton Av. NG24: N'wark T 7J 35
Ironestone Cl. NG24: Bald 1J 17
Ivies, The NG24: N'wark T 2A 36
Ivywood Cl. LN6: Lin 6E 14

J

Jacobean Rd. LN6: Lin 1H 21
Jaguar Dr. LN6: N Hyk 6H 21
Jalland's Row NG24: N'wark T 6E 34
James Cl. LN4: Welt 1C 4
James St. LN2: Lin 2C 38 (2F 17)
Jarvis Cl. LN6: Lin 7K 15
Jarvis Ho. LN6: Lin 7K 15
Jasmin Rd. LN6: Lin 6G 15
Jason Rd. LN6: Lin 2A 22
Jellicoe Av. LN2: Lin 2K 17
Jenison Ho. NG24: N'wark T 4D 36
Jensen Rd. LN4: Brac B 5F 23
Jericho Rd. NG24: Bald 6H 37
Jermyn M. LN4: Wash 5F 19
Jersey St. NG24: N'wark T 3C 36
JERUSALEM 3D 14
Jerusalem LN6: Skel 5D 14
Jerusalem Cotts. LN6: Skel 4D 14
Jerusalem Rd. LN6: Skel 3D 14
Jesmond Vw. LN1: Lin 5E 10
Jessop Cl. LN3: C Will 1G 19
Jessop Way NG24: N'wark T 6G 35
Jew's House 3C 38 (2F 17)
John Gold Av. NG24: N'wark T 1F 37
John Pope Way NG24: N'wark T 3F 35
Johns Cl. LN2: Welt 1C 4
Johnson Dr. LN4: Brac B 4F 23
Johnsons La. LN6: N Hyk 5J 21
Johnsons Rd. NG24: Bald 6K 37
Johnson Vs. LN4: Bran 3E 24
John St. LN2: Lin 3G 17
Jubilee Cl. LN3: C Will 7G 13
　　LN6: N Hyk 6K 21
Jubilee Ct. LN2: Nett 1C 12
Jubilee Dr. LN8: Wrag 4G 7
Jubilee Rd. NG24: N'wark T 1E 36
Julia Rd. LN4: Wash 5F 19
Juniper Cl. LN4: Bran 3E 24
　　LN5: Lin .5C 22
Juniper Dr. LN2: Scot 7G 5
Junxion, The LN5: Lin 6B 38 (4E 16)

K

Karglen Ind. Est. LN4: Bran 5J 25
Karsons Way LN2: Welt 1D 4
Keadby Cl. LN6: Lin 7K 15
Keats Cl. LN2: Lin 6J 11
Keats Rd. NG24: Bald 3H 37
Keddington Av. LN1: Lin 5E 10
Keeble Dr. LN4: Wash 5F 19
Keepers Cl. LN2: Welt 1C 4
Kelham La. NG23: S Mus 2A 34
　　NG24: N'wark T 4B 34
Kelham Rd. NG23: N'wark T 4A 34
　　NG24: N'wark T 6C 34
　　　　　　　　　　　　　　　(Cullen Cl.)
　　NG24: N'wark T 4A 34
　　　　　　　　　　　　　　　(Kelham La.)
Kells Cl. LN5: Lin 4D 22
Kelsey St. LN1: Lin 5B 38 (3E 16)
Kelstern Cl. LN6: Lin 1G 21
Kelstern Rd. LN6: Lin 1G 21
Kemble Cl. LN6: Lin 6F 15
Kendall Cl. LN2: Scot 1H 13
Kenilworth Cl. LN1: Sax 2E 8
Kenilworth Dr. LN6: Lin 2C 22
Kennedy Rd. LN4: Brac B 4F 23
Kennedy Wlk. NG24: Bald 4J 37
Kennel La. LN3: Ree 4F 13
　　LN6: Dodd 5A 14
Kennel Wlk. LN3: Ree 5H 13
Kenner Cl. LN6: Lin 1A 22
Kenneth St. LN1: Lin 7F 11

Kennington Cl. LN2: Dunh 4E 4
Kensington Ho. LN2: Lin 6G 11
Kent St. LN2: Lin 3J 17
Kenyon Cl. LN4: H'ton 7F 19
Kerrison Vw. LN2: Nett 1C 12
Kershaw Vw. LN1: Lin 5D 10
Kesteven Ct. LN6: N Hyk 5H 21
　　　　　　　　　　　　　　(not continuous)
Kesteven St. LN5: Lin 7C 38 (4F 17)
　　　　　　　　　　　　　　(not continuous)
Kestrel Cl. LN6: Lin 6H 15
Kew Gdns. NG24: New B 4F 37
Kexby Mill Cl. LN6: N Hyk 7H 21
Khormaksar Dr. LN4: Noct 6C 28
Kilburn Cres. LN6: Lin 1A 22
Kilminster Ct. LN8: Wrag 3G 7
Kinder Av. LN6: N Hyk 5A 22
King Dr. LN4: Brac B 5H 23
Kingfisher Cl. LN6: Lin 6H 15
　　NG24: New B 4G 37
Kings Arms Yd. LN2: Lin 4C 38 (3F 17)
Kingsdown Rd. LN6: Lin 7F 15
Kingsley Cl. LN4: Pott 2B 28
Kingsley Rd. LN6: Lin 2F 21
Kingsley St. LN1: Lin 1A 38 (1E 16)
Kingsnorth Cl. NG24: N'wark T 7E 34
Kings Rd. LN4: Meth 4G 29
　　NG24: N'wark T 6D 34
Kings Sconce Av.
　　NG24: N'wark T 4E 34
King St. LN5: Lin 7B 38 (4E 16)
　　NG24: N'wark T 1C 36
Kings Way LN4: Welt 1B 4
Kingsway LN2: Nett 2A 12
　　LN5: Lin .5F 17
　　NG24: New B 4G 37
Kinloss Cl. LN6: Lin 1G 21
Kipling Cl. LN2: Lin 6H 11
Kirkby St. LN5: Lin 5F 17
Kirk Ga. NG24: N'wark T 6D 34
Kirkstall Cl. LN2: Lin 7A 12
Kirmington Cl. LN6: Lin 1F 21
Kirton Cl. NG24: Bald 6H 37
Kneeland LN2: Dunh 3D 4
Knight Pl. LN5: Lin 6E 16
Knight's Ct. NG24: N'wark T 7E 34
Knight St. LN5: Lin 6E 16
Knight Ter. LN5: Lin 5E 16
Knipton Cl. NG24: Bald 5H 37
Knott's Ct. NG24: Bald 4H 37

L

Laburnum Cl. LN4: Bran 3E 24
　　LN6: N Hyk 5K 21
　　NG24: New B 3G 37
Laburnum Ct. LN3: Ree 5J 13
Laburnum Dr. LN3: C Will 2F 19
Laceby St. LN2: Lin 3H 17
Lacey Grn. NG24: Bald 5J 37
Lacy Cl. LN2: Nett 2D 12
Ladd's Mill Cl. LN6: N Hyk 7H 21
Lady Bower Cl. LN6: N Hyk 5A 22
Lady Elizabeth Ct. LN2: Dunh 3E 4
Lady Meers Rd. LN3: C Will 7G 13
LA Fitness
　　Lincoln, Weaver Rd. 2F 21
　　Lincoln, Witham Pk. Ho. 4G 17
　　Newark-on-Trent 5F 35
Lagonda Cl. LN4: Brac B 5F 23
Lakeside Cen. NG24: New B 3G 37
Lake Vw. Cl. LN6: N Hyk 6G 21
Lake Vw. Rd. LN6: Lin 1C 22
Lamb Cl. NG24: N'wark T 2A 36
Lamb Gdns. LN2: Lin 6H 11
Lancaster Cl. LN5: Wad 3G 27
　　　　　　　　　　　　　　(not continuous)
Lancaster Ct. LN2: Welt 2C 4
Lancaster Pl. LN5: Lin 5F 17
Lancaster Rd. NG24: Codd 5J 35
Lancaster Way LN6: Skel 2D 14
Lancewood Gdns. LN6: Lin 6G 15
Lancia Cres. LN4: Brac B 5F 23
Landings, The LN1: B Wat 7J 9
Landmere Gro. LN6: Lin 5H 15
Laney Cl. LN2: Lin 6J 11

Langdale Cl. LN2: Lin 4H 11
NG24: N'wark T 4C 36
Langer Cl. LN6: Lin 1F 21
Langford La. NG23: Holm 3D 32
Langley Rd. LN6: N Hyk 5H 21
LANGTON BY WRAGBY 6K 7
Langton Cl. LN2: Lin 6H 11
LANGWORTH 5C 6
Langworthgate LN2: Lin 2E 38 (2G 17)
Langworth Rd. LN2: Scot 6J 5
Lannimore Cl. LN5: Lin 4D 22
Lansbury Rd. NG24: New B 4G 37
Lansdowne Av. LN6: Lin 2C 22
Lansdowne Rd. LN5: Nav 4J 31
Lapwing Cl. LN6: Skel 3E 14
Larch Av. LN2: Nett 2D 12
Larchwood Cres. LN6: Lin 6G 15
Lark Cl. LN8: Wrag 4G 7
Lark Dr. LN5: Well 6J 31
Larkin Av. LN3: C Will 1F 19
Larkspur Rd. LN2: Lin 5K 11
Larne Cl. LN5: Lin 5C 22
Larne Rd. LN5: Lin 4D 22
Laughton Cres. LN2: Lin 5G 11
Laughton Way LN2: Lin 5G 11
Laughton Way Nth. LN2: Lin 5F 11
Laurel Cl. LN5: Lin 2D 22
Lavender Cl. LN5: Lin 5C 22
Lavenham Gro. LN6: Lin 3A 22
Lawley Cl. LN2: N Gre 5D 12
Lawn Cotts. LN1: Lin 1B 38 (1E 16)
Lawn Ct. LN1: Lin 1B 38 (1E 16)
Lawns, The NG23: Coll 3J 33
Lawrence Cl. NG24: N'wark T 7B 16
Lawrence Pl. NG24: N'wark T 6E 34
Lawrence St. NG24: N'wark T 6E 34
Lawson Ct. LN2: Dunh 3F 5
Leach's Bldgs. NG24: N'wark T 1C 36
Lealand Cl. LN2: Lin 7A 12
Learoyd Ho. LN2: Lin 5H 11
Lechler Cl. LN2: Nett 1B 12
Leconfield Cl. LN6: Lin 1G 21
Leconfield Rd. LN6: Lin 7G 15
Lee Av. LN4: H'ton, Wash 6F 19
Leeming Cl. LN6: Lin 1H 21
Lee Rd. LN2: Lin 7G 11
Legbourne Cl. LN1: Lin 6D 10
Le Grand Luce Ct. LN3: C Will 7G 13
Leicester Cl. LN4: Wash 5E 18
Leighton Cres. LN6: Lin 1A 22
Lenton Grn. LN2: Lin 6H 11
Lenton Ter. NG24: N'wark T 7C 34
Levellers Way NG24: N'wark T 7J 35
Leveret Chase LN6: With S 6B 26
Lewis St. LN5: Lin 7C 38 (4F 17)
Lexington Ho. LN5: Lin 2D 22
Leyburn Rd. LN6: Lin 3K 21
Ley La. LN5: Bass 5E 30
Leys, The LN3: C Will 7G 13
Ley's Cl. LN6: N Hyk 5H 21
Lichfield Rd. LN4: Brac B 3G 23
Lievelsley Rd. LN1: Lin 7D 10
Lightfoot Cl. NG24: N'wark T 7J 35
Lilac Cl. LN6: Lin 6G 15
NG24: N'wark T 4D 36
Lilburne Cl. NG24: N'wark T 7J 35
Lilford Cl. LN2: Lin 6A 12
Lilford Rd. LN2: Lin 6A 12
Lillicrap Ct. LN1: Lin 1B 38 (1E 16)
Lilly's Rd. LN1: Lin 1C 38 (1F 17)
Limeberry Pl. LN6: Lin 6E 14
Lime Cres. LN5: Wad 6C 22
Lime Gro. LN3: C Will 1F 19
LN5: Bass 3D 30
NG24: N'wark T 1D 36
Lime Kiln Way LN2: Lin 2J 17
Limelands LN2: Lin 2G 17
Lime Tree Av. LN4: Meth 4H 29
Lime Tree Cl. LN6: Lin 6J 15
NG23: Coll 4H 33
Lime Tree Paddock LN2: Scot 6H 5
LINCOLN 4C 38 (3F 17)
Lincoln Arboretum 2G 17
Lincoln Av. LN6: Lin 6C 16
Lincoln Bowl 5J 17
Lincoln Bus. Pk. LN6: Lin 2F 21
Lincoln Castle 2B 38 (2E 16)

Lincoln Cathedral 2D 38 (2F 17)
Lincoln Central Station (Rail) ..6C 38 (4F 17)
Lincoln City FC 5E 16
Lincoln Corn Exchange LN5: Lin 5C 38
LINCOLN COUNTY HOSPITAL 2H 17
Lincoln Ct. NG24: N'wark T 4F 35
Lincoln Dr. LN5: Wad 2G 27
(not continuous)
Lincoln Golf Range 5J 17
Lincoln La. LN6: T Hill 7A 20
Lincoln Lawn Tennis & Bowls Club ...1E 38
LINCOLN NUFFIELD HOSPITAL
.........................1D 38 (1F 17)
Lincoln Relief Rd. LN2: Lin 4F 11
LN6: Lin, Skel, S Hyk 5D 20
Lincoln Rd. LN1: Sax 3G 9
LN2: Dunh 4D 4
LN2: Lin, Nett 5J 11
LN2: Welt, Dunh 2C 4
LN3: Fis 2H 19
LN4: Bran, Can 7H 17
LN4: Duns 2F 29
LN4: Meth 5G 29
LN4: Wash 4B 18
LN5: Bass 3C 30
LN6: Dodd 6A 14
LN6: N Hyk 6K 21
LN6: Skel 3E 14
NG24: N'wark T 4F 35
Lincoln Rd. Bri. NG24: N'wark T 5E 34
Lincoln Road Farm 3G 15
Lincoln Rd. Nocton LN4: Duns, Noct ..7A 28
Lincolnshire Road Transport Mus. 2H 21
Lincoln Shop. Cen. LN6: Lin 4D 16
Lincoln St. NG24: N'wark T 5E 34
Lincoln W. Retail Pk. LN6: Lin 5C 16
Lincoln YMCA Fitness Cen. 5E 38
Linden Av. LN4: Bran 3D 24
NG24: New B 2F 37
Linden Ct. LN4: Brac B 5G 23
Lindholme Rd. LN6: Lin 1H 21
Lindrick Cl. LN4: H'ton 6F 19
Lindsay Av. NG24: N'wark T 4D 36
Lindum Av. LN2: Lin 3E 38 (2G 17)
Lindum Bus. Pk. LN6: N Hyk 3H 21
Lindum Ct. LN4: Brac B 5G 23
Lindum M. NG24: N'wark T 7E 34
Lindum Rd. LN2: Lin 4D 38 (2F 17)
Lindum Sports Club 1E 38 (1G 17)
Lindum St. NG24: N'wark T 7E 34
Lindum Ter. LN2: Lin 3E 38 (2G 17)
Linga La. LN5: Bass 2D 30
Lingfield Cl. LN1: Sax 1E 8
Linley Cl. NG23: Coll 4H 33
Linnet Cl. LN6: Lin 6H 15
Linseed Av. NG24: N'wark T 3F 35
Lintin Cl. LN4: H'ton 7F 19
Linton St. LN5: Lin 5F 17
Lisburn Cl. LN5: Lin 5D 22
Lissett Cl. LN6: Lin 1F 21
Lissington Cl. LN2: Lin 6F 11
Lit. Bargate St. LN5: Lin 6E 16
LITTLE CARLTON 1A 34
Lit. Gate La. LN4: Pott 6J 25
Little La. NG23: Coll 5G 33
Lit. Thorpe La. LN6: T Hill 7B 20
Liverpool Dr. LN6: Skel 4F 15
Locking Cl. LN6: Lin 1G 21
Lodge Cl. LN2: Welt 1C 4
LN6: Lin 2J 21
Lodge Dr. LN4: Bran 4F 25
Lodge La. LN2: Nett 2D 12
Lombard St. NG24: N'wark T 7D 34
Londesborough Way LN4: N'wark 5J 29
Londinium Way LN6: N Hyk 7H 21
London Rd. LN4: Brac B 2F 23
LN4: Bald, New B, N'wark T 7D 34
Longacre Pk. LN6: S Hyk 6E 20
Longdales Rd. LN2: Lin 7F 11
Long Hollow Way NG24: Wint 3H 35
Longhurst LN6: Lin 6F 15
Longland Wlk. LN2: Lin 6K 11
Long Leys Rd. LN1: Lin 1A 38 (6A 10)
Long Row NG24: N'wark T 7F 35

Longstongs Cres. LN4: Wash 4E 18
Long Wood La. LN4: Blank 7H 29
Lonsdale Ct. LN4: Wash 5D 18
Lonsdale Pl. LN5: Lin 5F 17
Lotus Cl. LN5: Wad 2F 27
Lotus Ct. LN6: N Hyk 6H 21
Louth Rd. LN8: Wrag 3G 7
Loveden Cl. NG24: Bald 5H 37
Lover's La. NG24: N'wark T 6E 34
Lwr. Church Rd. LN6: Skel 2F 15
Lwr. High St. LN5: Wad 2F 27
Lowfield Cotts. NG24: New B 5E 36
Lowfield La. NG24: Bald, New B 5F 37
Lowfields Cen. LN5: Lin 5D 22
Low Moor Rd. LN6: Lin 2J 21
Low Pk. La. LN4: H'ton 6H 19
Low St. NG23: Coll 5G 33
Lucy Tower St. LN1: Lin 5B 38 (3E 16)
Ludford Dr. LN6: Lin 7A 16
Lumley Pl. LN5: Lin 5F 17
Lunn La. NG23: Coll 5G 33
Lupin Rd. LN2: Lin 5J 11
Lurgan Cl. LN5: Lin 4D 22
Luton Cl. LN6: Lin 5F 15
Lydd Cl. LN6: Lin 1G 21
Lyndon Bus. Pk. LN6: Lin 2F 21
Lyneham Cl. LN6: Lin 7F 15
Lynmouth Cl. LN6: N Hyk 6A 22
Lysterfield Ct. LN6: N Hyk 6G 21
Lytham Cl. LN4: H'ton 5F 19
Lytton St. LN2: Lin 3G 17

M

Macaulay Cl. NG24: Bald 3H 37
Macaulay Dr. LN2: Lin 7H 11
NG24: Bald 3H 37
McInnes St. LN2: Lin 3J 17
Mackleys La. NG23: N Mus 4C 32
Macmillan Av. LN6: N Hyk 6G 21
Macphail Cres. LN1: Sax 3G 9
Madden Cl. LN1: Lin 7C 10
Magdalene Vw. NG24: N'wark T 7F 35
Magnolia Cl. LN4: Bran 3D 24
Magnus St. NG24: N'wark T 6E 34
Magpie Cl. LN6: Skel 3E 14
Magpies Sq. LN2: Lin 5D 38
Maiden Ct. LN1: Sax 3F 9
Maidenwell Cl. LN5: Nav 4J 31
Maidenwell La. LN5: Nav 4H 31
Maidment Dr. LN1: Lin 6C 10
Main Av. LN4: Brac B 4F 23
Main Dr. LN2: Scot 1J 13
Main Rd. LN3: L'worth 4C 6
LN4: Noct 6B 28
LN4: Pott 2A 28
LN4: Wash 4D 18
Main St. LN1: Bur 3B 10
LN2: Scot 7G 5
LN5: Booth G 1H 31
LN6: Dodd 5A 14
LN6: T Hill 7B 20
NG23: N Mus 3C 32
NG23: S Mus 1B 34
NG24: Bald 4H 37
Mainwaring Cl. LN2: Dunh 3E 4
Mainwaring Rd. LN2: Lin 1E 38 (1G 17)
Malham Cl. LN6: Lin 5G 15
Malham Dr. LN6: Lin 4G 15
Mallard Cl. LN6: Lin 5J 15
LN6: Skel 3E 14
Mallard Ct. LN6: N Hyk 6G 21
Mallard Grn. NG24: New B 3G 37
Mallory Cl. LN6: Lin 7G 15
Mall Shop Cen., The LN2: Lin ...4C 38 (3F 17)
Malt Kiln Cotts. LN8: Wrag 3F 7
Malt Kiln La. LN5: Wad 4E 26
Maltkiln La. NG24: N'wark T 5E 34
Malton Rd. LN6: N Hyk 4K 21
Maltsters, The NG24: N'wark T 2A 36
Malus Cl. LN4: Bran 3D 24
Malvern Av. LN4: Wash 5F 19
Malvern Cl. LN5: Lin 3D 22
LN6: N Hyk 7J 21
Manby St. LN5: Lin 1D 22
Manchester Rd. LN5: Wad 3G 27

Manners Rd. NG24: Bald 5G 37
  NG24: N'wark T 6C 34
Manor Cl. LN2: Lin 1F 17
  LN4: Meth .5J 29
Manor Ct. LN2: Nett 2A 12
  LN2: Scot 1G 13
  LN2: Welt 2C 4
  LN4: Noct 5B 28
  LN5: Carl M 7C 30
Manor Dr. LN2: Scot 1G 13
  LN8: Wrag .4H 7
Manor Grounds LN6: Skel 2F 15
Manor Ho. Dr. NG23: N Mus 3C 32
Manor La. LN1: Bro 5E 8
  LN2: Welt 2C 4
  LN5: Carl M 7C 30
  LN5: Wad 3E 26
Mnr. Leas Cl. LN6: Lin 4B 22
Manor Paddocks LN5: Bass 4C 30
Manor Ri. LN3: Ree 5H 13
Manor Rd. LN1: Sax 2E 8
  LN2: Lin 1G 17
  LN4: Wash .5D 18
  LN6: N Hyk 6J 21
  NG23: Coll .4H 33
Manor Way LN2: Dunh 3E 4
Manrico Dr. LN1: Lin 6C 10
Manse Av. LN5: Lin 3D 22
Mansford Cl. LN2: Nett 1B 12
Manthorpe Ho. NG24: Bald 4K 37
Manthorpe Way NG24: Bald 4J 37
Manton Rd. LN2: Lin 6F 11
Maple Cl. LN4: Brac B 5H 23
  LN5: Wad 7C 22
Maple Ct. LN1: Sax 2D 8
Maple Dr. LN2: Scot 1H 13
  LN5: Bass 2E 30
Maple Gro. NG24: N'wark T 4D 36
Maple St. LN5: Lin 2D 22
Mapleton LN6: N Hyk 7G 21
Mareham Cl. LN4: Brac B 5G 23
Marham Cl. LN6: Lin 6F 15
Marigold Cl. LN2: Lin 5J 11
Marina Cl. LN5: Wad 4F 27
                  (Millers Rd.)
  LN5: Wad 2F 27
               (Vanwall Dr.)
Marine App. LN1: B Wat 7J 9
Marine Point Apartments LN1: B Wat . . .7J 9
Marine Wlk. LN1: B Wat 7J 9
Marjorie Av. LN6: Lin 6D 16
Market Pl. LN8: Wrag 4G 7
  NG24: N'wark T 7D 34
Market Rasen Rd. LN2: Dunh 3E 4
            (not continuous)
Markham Av. NG24: N'wark T 4F 35
Markwick Cl. NG24: N'wark T 7H 35
Marlborough Av. LN4: Wash 5E 18
Marlborough Cl. LN2: Lin 5J 11
  NG24: N'wark T 3B 36
Marlborough Ct. LN4: Wash 5D 18
  NG24: N'wark T 3B 36
Marlborough Ho. LN2: Lin 6H 11
Marles Cl. NG24: N'wark T 5G 35
Marlowe Dr. LN2: Lin 7H 11
  NG24: Bald 4J 37
Marne Gdns. LN1: Lin 7E 10
Marquis Av. NG24: Bald 5J 37
Marrat Cl. LN2: Lin 7K 11
Marrion Cl. NG24: Bald 6K 37
Marshall Ct. NG24: Bald 4J 37
Marsh La. NG23: N Mus 4C 32
Marston Cl. NG24: Bald 5G 37
Marston Moor Rd. NG24: N'wark T 7J 35
Martin Cl. LN4: H'ton 7F 19
  LN6: Skel 3E 14
Martin St. LN5: Lin 5F 17
Marton Rd. NG24: N'wark T 4J 37
Mary Sookias Ho. LN1: Lin 1C 38 (1F 17)
Masefield Cres. NG24: Bald 4H 37
Massey Rd. LN2: Lin 1G 17
Massey St. NG24: N'wark T 7F 35
Mather Rd. NG24: Bald 6D 34
Matilda Rd. LN6: Lin 5D 16
Matlock Dr. LN6: N Hyk 5J 21
Maun Grn. NG24: N'wark T 5F 35
Maxwell Av. LN6: Lin 6C 16

Mayall Ct. LN5: Wad 3F 27
Mayall Wlk. LN5: Wad 3F 27
May Cres. LN1: Lin 2D 16
Mayfair Av. LN6: Lin 7C 16
Mayfair Cl. LN3: C Will 6G 13
Mays La. LN1: Sax 3F 9
Maythorne Cl. NG24: New B 3G 37
Mead, The LN4: Meth 2A 22
Mead Cl. LN6: Lin 2A 22
Meadow Bank Av. LN3: Fis 3K 19
Meadow Cl. LN2: Scot 6H 5
  LN3: Ree 5J 13
  LN4: Meth .4J 29
  LN6: N Hyk 7K 21
  NG23: N Mus 5C 32
Meadow Farm Cvn. Site LN6: N Hyk 7K 21
Meadowlake Cl. LN6: Lin 5J 15
Meadow Lake Cres. LN6: Lin 5H 15
Meadow La. LN5: Wad 1A 26
  LN6: N Hyk . . . . .7K 21 & 1A 26
  LN6: S Hyk 3A 26
Meadow Ri. LN1: Sax 2F 9
Meadow Rd. LN4: Duns 2H 29
  NG24: New B 4G 37
Meadow Way LN2: Welt 2D 4
  LN4: Brac B 5G 23
Mead Way NG24: Bald 5F 37
Meadway LN3: C Will 7G 13
Medieval Bishop's Palace, The 3D 38
Medway Cres. LN6: N Hyk 5B 22
Meering Av. NG24: N'wark T 3F 35
Meering Cl. NG23: Coll 3H 33
Megs La. LN5: Nav 5J 31
Melbourne Cl. LN6: Lin 7G 15
Melbourne Rd. LN6: Lin 6G 15
Melbourne Way LN5: Wad 1C 26
Meldrum Cres. NG24: N'wark T 3C 36
Mellows Cl. LN3: Ree 5H 13
Melrose La. LN6: Lin 6F 15
Melville Cl. LN4: Bran 4E 24
Melville St. LN5: Lin 5D 38 (3F 17)
Memorial Hall Dr. LN5: Well 6H 31
Mendip Av. LN6: N Hyk 7J 21
Mendip Cl. LN5: Lin 4D 22
Mercer Dr. LN1: Lin 7D 10
Mercia Rd. NG24: N'wark T 3D 36
Mere Rd. LN4: Brac B, Bran 7D 24
  LN5: Wad 3F 27
Merleswen LN2: Dunh 3D 4
Merrycock La. LN4: H'ton 7F 19
METHERINGHAM 5H 29
Metheringham Cl. LN6: Lin 7H 15
Metheringham Fen La. LN4: Meth 4J 29
Metheringham Heath La. LN4: Meth 5F 29
Metheringham Station (Rail) 5K 29
Meynell Av. LN6: Lin 6C 16
Meyrick Rd. NG24: N'wark T 6E 34
Michaelgate LN1: Lin 3C 38 (2F 17)
Middlebrook Cl. LN6: Lin 2A 22
Middlebrook Rd. LN6: Lin 2K 21
Middle Ga. LN5: Bass 3D 30
  NG24: N'wark T 7D 34
Middle La. LN6: T Hill 7C 20
Middle St. LN1: Bur, S Car 1B 10
  LN4: Duns .2G 29
  LN4: Meth .5H 29
  LN4: Pott 2A 28
  LN6: N Hyk 7K 21
Middleton Rd. NG24: N'wark T 4F 35
Middleton's Fld. LN2: Lin 1D 38 (1F 17)
Middleway LN3: C Will 1G 19
Midholm LN3: C Will 1G 19
Midland St. LN1: Lin 6C 10
Midland Ter. NG24: N'wark T 6C 34
Midville Cl. LN1: Lin 5E 10
Midway Cl. LN2: Nett 1C 12
Midway Ct. LN2: Nett 1C 12
Mildenhall Dr. LN6: Lin 6F 15
Mildmay St. LN1: Lin 7E 10
Millbeck Dr. LN2: Lin 4G 11
Millbrook Cl. LN6: Lin 7H 21
Millbrook La. LN8: Wrag 4F 7
Mill Ct. LN1: Lin 1E 16
Millers Cl. LN4: H'ton 6E 18
Millers Dale LN6: N Hyk 5K 21
Millers Rd. LN5: Wad 4F 27
Millfield Av. LN1: Sax 2F 9
Millfield Rd. LN4: Meth 5G 29

Mill Flds. LN5: Bass 2D 30
Mill Ga. NG24: N'wark T 1C 36
Millgate LN5: Well 6H 31
Millgate Mus. .7C 34
Mill Grn. NG24: N'wark T 7F 35
Mill Ho. LN1: Lin 4A 38 (3E 16)
Mill La. LN1: Sax 2F 9
  LN4: H'ton .6F 19
  LN5: Lin 5E 16
  LN6: N Hyk 7H 21
  NG23: N Mus, S Mus 5B 32
             (not continuous)
  NG24: N'wark T 7C 34
Mill Mere Rd. LN5: Wad 2F 27
Mill Moor Way LN6: N Hyk 6H 21
Mill Ri. LN2: Scot 7H 5
  LN5: Well 6H 31
Mill Rd. LN1: Lin 1A 38 (1E 16)
Mill Row LN1: Lin 1E 16
Mills Dr. NG24: N'wark T 2A 36
Mill Stone La. LN5: Wad 2F 27
Millstream Rd. LN4: H'ton 6F 19
Mill Vw. Ct. LN8: Wrag 4G 7
Mill Vw. Rd. LN8: Wrag 4G 7
Milman Rd. LN2: Lin 3H 17
Milner St. NG24: N'wark T 1E 36
Milton Cl. LN3: C Will 1G 19
  LN4: Bran .3C 24
Milton St. LN5: Lin 1E 22
  NG24: New B 2F 37
Minster Cl. LN4: Brac B 3G 23
Minster Dr. LN3: C Will 6G 13
Minster Yd. LN2: Lin 2C 38 (2F 17)
             (not continuous)
Minting Cl. LN1: Lin 5E 10
Mint La. LN1: Lin 4B 38 (3E 16)
Mint St. LN1: Lin 4B 38 (3E 16)
Mitchel Dr. LN1: Lin 7C 10
Mitchell Cl. LN6: Skel 2E 14
Monce Cl. LN2: Welt 1B 4
Monckton Way LN2: Dunh 4D 4
Monks Leys Ter. LN2: Lin 2G 17
Monks Mnr. Ct. LN2: Lin 1H 17
Monks Mnr. Dr. LN2: Lin 2H 17
Monks Rd. LN2: Lin 4D 38 (3F 17)
Monks Way LN2: Lin 3K 17
Monkwood Cl. NG23: Coll 3J 33
Monsal Dale LN6: N Hyk 5K 21
Monson Cl. LN5: Lin 7B 38 (5E 16)
Monson Pk. LN6: Skel 2E 14
Monson St. LN5: Lin 7B 38 (5E 16)
Mons Rd. LN1: Lin 7E 10
Montague St. LN2: Lin 4E 38 (3G 17)
Montague Ter. LN2: Lin 4E 38 (3G 17)
Montagu Rd. LN4: Can 6H 17
Montaigne Cl. LN2: Lin 6K 11
Montaigne Cres. LN2: Lin 6K 11
Montaigne Gdn. LN2: Lin 6K 11
Montgomery Rd. NG24: N'wark T 3E 36
Montrose Cl. LN6: N Hyk 6J 21
Moorby Cl. LN1: Lin 6E 10
Moorhen Cl. LN6: With S 7A 26
Moorhouse La. NG23: S Mus 5A 32
Moorings, The LN1: B Wat 7J 9
Moorland Av. LN6: Lin 2A 22
Moorland Cen. LN6: Lin 2K 21
Moorland Cl. LN5: Carl M 7C 30
  LN6: Lin 2K 21
Moorland Cres. LN6: Lin 1B 22
Moorlands, The LN4: Meth 5K 29
Moorland Way LN6: Lin 2K 21
Moor La. LN3: Ree 4J 13
             (not continuous)
  LN4: Bran .4F 25
  LN4: Meth .5K 29
  LN4: Pott 2A 28
  LN6: N Hyk 6H 21
  LN6: T Hill .6A 20
  LN6: With S 7A 26
Moor Rd. NG23: Coll 3J 33
MOORS, THE .2J 25
Moorside Ct. LN6: N Hyk 7J 21
Moor St. LN1: Lin 2D 16
Morden Cl. LN4: Meth 5J 29
Morris Cl. LN2: Dunh 3E 4
Morton Dr. LN6: Lin 7K 15

Motherby Hill LN1: Lin 3B 38 (2E 16)
Motherby La. LN1: Lin 3B 38 (2E 16)
Moulton Cres. NG24: New B 5G 37
Mount, The NG24: N'wark T 6D 34
Mount Ct. NG24: Bald 4G 37
  NG24: N'wark T 6D 34
  (off Mount La.)
Mount La. NG24: N'wark T 7E 34
Mountney Pl. NG24: N'wark T 4F 35
Mount Rd. LN4: Brac B 4F 23
  NG24: Bald 4G 37
Mount St. LN1: Lin 7E 10
Mourn Ter. LN5: Lin 5D 22
Moxons La. LN5: Wad 3F 27
Much La. LN1: Lin 5B 38 (1E 16)
Muirfield Cl. LN6: Lin 7F 15
Mulberry Av. LN6: N Hyk 5K 21
Mulberry Cl. LN5: Wad 6C 22
Mumby Cl. NG24: N'wark T 6E 34
Muntjac Way LN6: With S 6A 26
Murdock Rd. LN6: Lin 1E 22
Murfin Ho. LN6: Lin 2B 22
Museum Ct. LN2: Lin 4C 38
Mus. of Lincolnshire Life 1A 38
Musgraves Orchard LN2: Welt 1E 4
Muskham La. NG23: Bath 4A 32
Muskham Vw. NG24: N'wark T 6D 34

N

Naam Gro. LN1: Lin 1B 38 (1E 16)
Naam Pl. LN1: Lin 1B 38 (1E 16)
Napier St. LN2: Lin 3H 17
Narrow Moor La. LN5: Bass 7K 7
  (not continuous)
Naseby Av. NG24: N'wark T 7J 35
Nash La. LN6: N Hyk 6J 21
Natal Vw. LN1: Lin 5D 10
NAVENBY 4J 31
Navenby Bowls Club 5J 31
Navenby La. LN5: Bass 5C 30
Navigation Yd. NG24: N'wark T 7C 34
Neale Ct. LN6: N Hyk 7J 21
Neale Rd. LN6: N Hyk 7J 21
Neile Cl. LN2: Lin 6K 11
Nelson Dr. LN4: Wash 4D 18
Nelson La. NG23: N Mus 4B 32
Nelson Rd. NG3: Fis . . . . .2K 19 & 4K 19
  NG24: New B 4F 37
Nelson St. LN1: Lin 3D 16
Nelthorpe St. LN5: Lin 7B 38 (5E 16)
Nene Pk. LN6: N Hyk 6G 21
Nene Rd. LN1: Lin 5E 10
NETTLEHAM .2B 12
Nettleham Cl. LN2: Lin 7G 11
Nettleham Rd. LN2: Lin 1D 38 (1F 17)
  LN2: Nett, Scot 7E 4
Nettleham Rd. Shop. Cen. LN2: Lin 5H 11
Nettleton Cl. LN4: Bran 3E 24
Nettleton Dr. LN6: With S 5C 26
Nettleton Ho. LN2: Lin 5H 11
Neustadt Ct. LN2: Lin 3C 38 (2F 17)
Neville Wlk. LN5: Well 6H 31
Newark Air Mus. 2K 35
Newark & Notts Gliding Club 2K 35
Newark Bus. Pk. NG24: N'wark T 6F 35
Newark Castle 6D 34
Newark Castle Station (Rail) 6D 34
Newark Golf Cen. (Driving Range) 2J 35
NEWARK HOSPITAL 2E 35
Newark Northgate Station (Rail) 5F 35
NEWARK-ON-TRENT 7D 34
Newark Rd. LN5: Bass 3C 30
  LN5: Lin .3A 22
  LN6: N Hyk, S Hyk 7E 20
  NG23: Coll 6G 33
  NG24: Codd 6J 35
  NG24: Hawt 5B 36
Newark Showground 2K 35
NEW BALDERTON 3G 37
NEWBALL 4E 6
NEW BOULTHAM 6A 38 (3D 16)
Newbury Rd. NG24: N'wark T 6J 35
Newcastle Av. NG24: N'wark T 2E 36
Newcot La. LN4: H'ton 7H 19
New Cres. LN3: C Will 7F 13

Newhaven Dr. LN5: Lin 4D 22
Newland LN1: Lin 4A 38 (3E 16)
Newland St. W. LN1: Lin 3A 38 (2D 16)
Newnham Rd. NG24: N'wark T 6E 34
Newport NG1: Lin 1C 38 (1F 17)
Newport Arch 1C 38
Newport Ct. LN1: Lin 1C 38 (1F 17)
Newport Cres. LN5: Wad 2F 27
Newporte Bus. Pk. LN2: Lin 1J 17
Newstead Av. LN3: C Will 1G 19
  NG24: N'wark T 6E 34
New St. NG24: N'wark T 7E 34
Newsums Vs. LN1: Lin 2C 16
New Ten Row LN4: Noct 6B 28
Newton Cl. LN4: Meth 4H 29
  LN8: Wrag .4H 7
Newton St. LN5: Lin 5D 38 (3F 17)
  NG24: N'wark T 1F 37
Newton Way LN3: C Will 7D 12
Nicholson Ct. NG24: N'wark T 1E 36
Nicholson St. NG24: N'wark T 1E 36
Nicholson's Wharf NG24: N'wark T 6D 34
Nightingale Cl. NG24: Bald 4J 37
Nightingale Cres. LN6: Lin 6H 15
Nixon Way NG23: Coll 3H 33
Noble Ho. NG24: N'wark T 4D 36
NOCTON 6B 28
Nocton Dr. LN2: Lin 5F 11
Nocton Fen La. LN4: Noct 4B 28
Nocton Pk. Rd. LN4: Noct 5B 28
Nocton Rd. LN4: Noct, Pott 3B 28
Norbeck La. LN2: Welt 2B 4
Norfolk Cres. LN4: Brac B 3F 23
Norfolk St. LN1: Lin 2C 16
Norman Av. NG24: N'wark T 3F 35
Norman Cl. LN4: Meth 5G 29
Norman St. LN5: Lin 6C 38 (4F 17)
Normanton Rd. NG24: N'wark T 6H 35
Norris St. LN5: Lin 5F 17
North Ct. LN2: Nett 1B 12
Northcroft NG1: Sax 1E 8
Northcroft La. NG23: Coll 2F 33
Nth. Dales Rd. LN4: Wash . . . . .4J 19 & 4K 19
North Dr. NG24: Bald 6J 37
Northern Rd. NG24: N'wark T 5F 35
Northfield Av. LN2: Scot 1H 13
Northfield Ri. LN1: Sax 2D 8
Northfield Rd. LN2: Welt 1D 4
North Ga. NG24: N'wark T 6D 34
  (not continuous)
Northgate LN2: Lin 1D 38 (1F 17)
Northgate Retail Pk. NG24: N'wark T 5E 34
NORTH GREETWELL 5C 12
NORTH HYKEHAM 5H 21
Northing La. LN2: Scot 5H 5
North Kesteven Sports Cen. 6H 21
North La. LN3: Ree 4G 13
  LN5: Nav .4J 31
NORTH MUSKHAM 4C 32
Northorpe Cl. LN6: Lin 7K 15
North Pde. LN1: Lin 3A 38 (2E 16)
North St. LN2: Nett 1B 12
North Way LN6: N Hyk 5H 21
Norton Disney Rd. LN5: Carl M 5A 30
Norton La. LN6: With S 7A 26
Norwich Cl. LN4: Wash 5G 19
Norwich Dr. LN4: Brac B 4G 23
Nottingham Ter. LN2: Lin 3E 38 (2G 17)
Novona Ho. LN2: Lin 7K 11
Nursery Cl. LN1: Sax 2E 8
  LN2: Dunh .3F 5
  LN2: L'worth 5B 6
Nursery Ct. NG24: N'wark T 6E 34
Nursery Gro. LN2: Lin 7G 11
Nurses La. LN6: Skel 1E 14

O

Oak Av. LN2: Dunh 3E 4
Oak Cl. LN2: Scot 1H 13
Oak Cres. LN3: C Will 1F 19
Oakdene Av. LN4: Brac B 5G 23
Oak Dr. NG24: New B 3G 37
Oak Farm Paddock LN6: N Hyk 6G 21
Oakfield LN1: Sax 2E 8

Oakfield Rd. NG24: Bald 7K 37
Oakfield St. LN2: Lin 3H 17
Oak Hill LN4: Wash 4D 18
Oakland Cl. LN1: Lin 6D 10
Oaklands LN1: Sax 2E 8
  LN4: Bran .4F 25
  NG23: Coll 4H 33
Oaklands, The LN8: Wrag 4H 7
Oaklands Cl. NG23: Coll 5H 33
Oakleigh Dr. LN1: Lin 7C 10
Oakleigh Ter. LN1: Lin 7C 10
Oaks, The LN2: Nett 2D 12
  LN2: Scot .7G 5
  NG24: New B 4G 37
Oak Tree Dr. LN6: With S 7A 26
Oak Vw. LN2: Dunh 3E 4
Oakwood Av. LN6: Lin 6G 15
Oakwood Cl. LN3: C Will 1G 19
Oakwood Rd. LN6: Lin 1F 21
Oberon Cl. LN1: Lin 7C 10
Occupation La. LN1: Bro 6E 8
Occupation Rd. LN1: Lin 1B 38 (1E 16)
ODDER 4J 9
Odeon Cinema
  Lincoln 5B 38
Old Brickkiln La. LN5: Bass 4D 30
Old Brickyard, The LN5: Lin 4D 22
Old Chapel Rd. LN6: Skel 2E 14
Old Cobham Orchard NG24: New B 3F 37
Old Grammar School Way LN8: Wrag 3G 7
Old Hall Gdns. NG24: Codd 6K 35
Old Mill, The LN5: Lin 5D 16
Old Mill Cres. NG24: N'wark T 7F 35
Old Oak Ri. LN6: Skel 2F 15
Old Palace, The LN2: Lin 3D 38
Old Pond Cl. LN6: Lin 6H 15
Old Rectory Ct. NG24: Wint 1G 35
Old Stack Yd., The LN4: H'ton 6G 19
Old Ten Row LN4: Noct 6B 28
Old Vicarage Gdns. LN6: Skel 3F 15
Old Wood Cl. LN6: Lin 5G 15
Oliver Cl. NG24: N'wark T 7F 35
Olive St. LN1: Lin 7E 10
Ollerton Rd. NG23: Lit C 1A 34
Olsen Cl. LN2: Lin 7K 11
Olsen Ri. LN2: Lin 7K 11
Orchard, The LN4: Wash 4C 18
  NG24: N'wark T 2F 37
Orchard Cl. LN2: Scot 7H 5
  LN2: Welt .2D 4
  LN3: C Will 1F 19
  LN4: Duns .1H 29
  LN4: Meth .5H 29
  LN5: Bass .2D 30
  LN6: Lin 7F 15
  NG23: S Mus 7B 32
Orchard Gth. LN5: Wad 1D 26
Orchard La. LN1: Sax 2E 8
Orchard Pk. NG24: Codd 5K 35
Orchard Rd. LN3: Fis 1K 19
Orchard St. LN1: Lin 4A 38 (3E 16)
Orchard Wlk. LN5: Brac B 1E 22
Orchard Way LN2: Nett 1C 12
  NG24: Bald 5H 37
Orchid Cl. NG24: New B 3F 37
Orchid Rd. LN5: Lin 5C 22
Ordoyno Gro. NG24: Codd 5K 35
Orston Av. NG24: N'wark T 2C 36
Osborne Cl. LN1: Lin 7E 10
Osiers, The NG24: N'wark T 2A 36
Ossington Way NG24: N'wark T 6D 34
Otter Av. LN1: Sax 2E 8
Otter Bank NG24: N'wark T 5E 34
Otters Cotts. LN5: Lin 7D 16
Oulton Cl. LN6: N Hyk 5A 22
Oundle Cl. LN4: Wash 5E 18
Outer Circ. Dr. LN2: Lin 6H 11
Outer Circ. Grn. LN2: Lin 7J 11
Outer Circ. Rd. LN2: Lin 7K 11
Oval, The LN2: Lin 6H 11
Oval App. LN2: Lin 6H 11
  (not continuous)
Overton Cl. LN5: Nav 4J 31
Owl Cl. LN6: With S 6A 26
Owls End LN2: Welt 1E 4
Oxeney Dr. LN3: L'worth 5C 6
Oxen Pk. Cl. LN2: Lin 4G 11

Oxford Cl.—Reepham Rd.

Oxford Cl. LN4: Wash 5E 18
Oxford St. LN5: Lin 6C 38 (4F 17)

P

Pach Way NG24: Bald 6K 37
Paddock, The LN2: Scot 2H 13
LN3: C Will 7G 13
LN4: Can 6H 17
LN6: Skel 2E 14
NG23: Coll 5H 33
Paddock Cl. LN4: Brac B 5G 23
Paddock La. LN4: Bran 4E 24
LN4: Meth 4H 29
Paddocks, The LN4: Pott 1A 28
NG24: N'wark T 1F 37
Padley Rd. LN2: Lin 7K 11
Painshall Cl. LN2: Welt 1C 4
Palace Theatre 7E 34
Palatine Ho. LN2: Lin 7K 11
Palmer St. LN5: Lin 7D 38 (5F 17)
Parade, The LN3: C Will 7G 13
Paradise Row LN6: Dodd 6A 14
Park, The LN1: Lin 4B 38 (3E 16)
LN4: Pott 3A 28
NG23: N Mus 3C 32
NG24: N'wark T 2E 36
Park Av. LN4: Wash 4E 18
LN6: Lin 6K 15
Park Cl. LN2: Scot 1H 13
Park Ct. LN1: Lin 4B 38 (3E 16)
Park Cres. LN4: Meth 5K 29
LN4: Wash 5E 18
NG24: N'wark T 4F 35
Parker Av. LN5: Lin 3D 22
Parker Cres. LN5: Lin 3D 22
Parker St. NG24: N'wark T 7E 34
Park Hill LN3: C Will 1G 19
Parkland Mobile Homes LN5: Wad 3G 27
Parklands Av. LN4: Noct 5B 28
Parklands Cl. NG24: Codd 5K 35
Parkland Way LN8: Wrag 4F 7
Park La. LN1: B Wat 6J 9
LN4: Brac B 3G 23
LN4: H'ton 6G 19
LN4: Wash 5E 18
LN5: Lin 1D 22
Parksgate Av. LN6: Lin 2K 21
Parkside LN2: Nett 2C 12
Park St. LN1: Lin 4B 38 (3E 16)
Parkview Apartments LN6: N Hyk 6J 21
Park Vw. Av. LN4: Bran 3C 24
Parkview Ct. LN4: Brac B 4F 23
Parkway NG24: N'wark T 2C 36
Parliament Ct. NG24: N'wark T 7C 34
Parliament St. NG24: N'wark T 7C 34
Parliament Wlk. *NG24: N'wark T 1C 36*
(off Parliament St.)
Partridge Grn. LN6: With S 6A 26
Pastures, The LN2: Welt 2D 4
Patch Rd. LN6: With S 7B 26
Pateley Moor Cl. LN6: N Hyk 7J 21
Pavilions, The LN1: Lin 6D 10
Pavilions Student Village, The
LN6: Lin 3D 16
Paving Way LN6: Lin 3G 21
Paxtons Ct. NG24: N'wark T 6D 34
Paynell LN2: Dunh 3D 4
Peak Dale LN6: N Hyk 5J 21
Pear Tree Cl. LN6: Lin 5G 15
Peddars Ct. LN4: Brac B 5G 23
Peebles Rd. NG24: N'wark T 3B 36
Peel St. LN5: Lin 5E 16
Peets Dr. NG23: N Mus 4C 32
Pelham Bri. LN5: Lin 6D 38 (4F 17)
Pelham Cl. LN2: Scot 1H 13
NG24: N'wark T 7C 34
Pelham Gdns. NG24: N'wark T 7D 34
Pelham La. LN4: Can 6H 17
Pelham St. LN5: Lin 6D 38 (4F 17)
NG24: N'wark T 7C 34
Pembertons Pl. LN3: Ree 4H 13
Pembrey Cl. LN6: Lin 7G 15
Pembroke Cres. NG24: N'wark T 4G 35
Pendennis LN5: Lin 1E 22
Pendine Cres. LN6: N Hyk 6A 22
Pendred Av. LN6: With S 7B 26
Penfold La. LN4: Wash 4E 18
Pennell St. LN5: Lin 5E 16
Pennycress Cl. LN2: Lin 5J 11
Penrose Cl. LN6: N Hyk 7J 21
Penswick Gro. NG24: Codd 5K 35
Pentland Dr. LN6: N Hyk 7J 21
Peppercorn Cl. LN6: Lin 5D 16
Percy St. LN2: Lin 3H 17
Perney Cres. LN6: N Hyk 7J 21
Perry Ct. LN4: Brac B 3F 23
Pershore Way LN6: Lin 1G 21
Peterborough Rd. NG23: Coll 3H 33
Peter Hodgkinson Cen. LN2: Lin 2J 17
Petersfield Cl. LN6: Lin 7F 15
Philip Ct. LN6: N Hyk 6K 21
Philip Rd. NG24: N'wark T 3C 36
Phillips Cl. LN2: Welt 1C 4
Phillpotts Cl. NG24: N'wark T 7H 35
Phipp's Pk. LN1: Lin 5D 10
Photinia Cl. LN4: Bran 3E 24
Pierson St. NG24: N'wark T 3C 36
Pietermaritz St. LN1: Lin 5E 10
Pietermaritz Vw. LN1: Lin 5E 10
Pigot Way LN2: Lin 7K 11
Pine Cl. LN1: Lin 5F 11
LN5: Wad 7C 22
NG24: Bald 7K 37
NG24: N'wark T 3F 35
Pinewood Cres. LN6: Lin 6F 15
Pinfold Cl. NG23: Coll 3H 33
Pinfold La. NG24: Bald 5H 37
Pinford Cl. LN5: Bass 2D 30
Pingle La. LN5: Well 7J 31
Pioneer Way LN6: Lin 3J 21
Pippin Ct. NG24: N'wark T 5F 35
Pitcairn Av. LN2: Lin 7K 11
Pitts Rd. LN4: Wash 5E 18
Platts, The NG24: N'wark T 2C 36
Pleasant Ter. *LN5: Lin 6E 16*
(off Sidney St.)
Plough La. LN3: Fis 1K 19
LN3: Ree 5H 13
Ploughmans Ct. LN2: Lin 7A 12
Ploughmans La. LN2: Lin 7A 12
Ploughmans Wlk. *LN2: Lin 7A 12*
(off Ploughmans Ct.)
Plover Gro. LN6: Lin 6J 15
Plum Way NG24: Bald 6J 37
Poachers Brook LN6: Skel 1E 14
Poachers Ct. LN1: Sax 3E 8
Poachers Mdw. LN2: Nett 2C 12
Poachers Rest LN2: Welt 1C 4
Pocklington Cres. NG24: Wint 1H 35
Pocklington Rd. NG23: Coll 3J 33
Point, The LN6: Lin 2F 21
Policemans La. LN4: Wash 4E 18
Pompeii Ct. LN6: N Hyk 7H 21
Pond Cl. LN2: Welt 3C 4
NG24: Bald 6K 37
Poplar Av. LN6: Lin 3C 16
Poplar Ct. LN6: Lin 3B 22
Poplar St. LN5: Lin 2D 22
Poppleton Ho. *LN6: Lin 3D 16*
(off The Pavilions Student Village)
Portland Ct. NG24: N'wark T 7D 34
Portland St. LN5: Lin 7B 38 (4E 16)
NG24: N'wark T 7D 34
Pottergate 3D 38 (2G 17)
Pottergate LN2: Lin 2D 38 (2F 17)
Pottergate Cl. LN5: Wad 2F 27
Pottergate Rd. LN5: Nav, Well 7J 31
POTTERHANWORTH 2A 28
POTTERHANWORTH HEATH 7G 25
Potterhanworth Rd. LN4: Bran, H'ton 7G 19
LN4: Noct 6B 28
Potter Hill Rd. NG23: Coll 5J 33
Prebend La. LN2: Welt 1B 4
Prenton Cl. LN6: Lin 2A 22
Preston Rd. NG24: N'wark T 7J 35
Prestwick Cl. LN6: Lin 5F 15
Prial Av. LN6: Lin 1B 22
Prial Cl. LN6: Lin 1B 22
Primrose Av. NG24: N'wark T 3F 35
Primrose Cl. LN5: Lin 5C 22
LN6: N Hyk 7F 21
Prince Charles Av. LN8: Wrag 4G 7
Princess Margaret Av. LN4: Meth 5H 29
Princess Royal Cl. LN2: Lin 2G 17
Princess St. LN5: Lin 5D 16
Prince's St. LN4: Meth 5G 29
NG24: N'wark T 1D 36
Prior La. LN4: Duns 1K 29
Prior St. LN5: Lin 7B 38 (5E 16)
Priory Cl. NG24: Bald 5H 37
Priory Dr. LN3: Fis 4K 19
Priorygate 2D 38 (2F 17)
Priory Ga. LN2: Lin 2D 38 (2F 17)
Priory Ho. LN5: Lin 7E 16
Private St. NG24: N'wark T 7F 35
Privet Wlk. LN6: With S 7A 26
Proctor M. *LN6: Lin 3D 16*
(off The Pavilions Student Village)
Proctors Rd. LN2: Lin 1K 17
Providence Row LN3: L'worth 5C 6
Pudding Busk La. LN4: H'ton 1F 25
Pullan Cl. LN5: Lin 4D 22
Pullman Cl. LN4: Meth 5K 29
Putnam Dr. LN2: Lin 7K 11
Pyke Rd. LN6: Lin 2H 21
Pynder Cl. LN4: Wash 4C 18

Q

Quarry Ind. Est., The LN5: Wad 2F 27
Queen Elizabeth Rd. LN1: Lin 5D 10
Queen Elizabeth St. LN8: Wrag 3G 7
Queen Headland La. LN5: Bass 5D 30
Queen Mary Rd. LN1: Lin 5D 10
Queensbury Ct. LN4: Wash 4D 18
Queen's Ct. NG24: N'wark T 6E 34
Queens Cres. LN1: Lin 1A 38 (1D 16)
Queens Farm Gdns. NG24: Bald 5H 37
Queen's Head Ct. NG24: N'wark T 7D 34
Queen's Rd. NG24: N'wark T 6D 34
Queen St. LN5: Lin 5E 16
NG23: Coll 3H 33
NG24: Bald 5J 37
NG24: N'wark T 1C 36
Queensway LN1: Sax 3F 9
LN2: Lin 1H 17
LN4: Pott 1B 28
LN6: Skel 3D 14
Queensway Ct. LN1: Sax 3F 9
Quibell Rd. NG24: N'wark T 3E 36
Quibell's La. NG24: N'wark T 4E 34
Quintin Cl. LN4: Brac B 4F 23
Quorn Dr. LN6: Lin 6C 16

R

Raglan Ct. NG24: N'wark T 1E 36
Raglan Gdns. NG24: N'wark T 1E 36
Railway Ct. LN1: Sax 3E 8
Railway Pk. Cl. LN6: Lin 5D 16
Railway Pk. M. LN6: Lin 5D 16
Randall Cl. NG24: N'wark T 7H 35
Ransome Cl. NG24: N'wark T 7H 35
Rasen La. LN1: Lin 1B 38 (1E 16)
Rauceby Ter. LN1: Lin 4A 38 (3E 16)
Ravendale Dr. LN2: Lin 6G 11
Ravensmoor Cl. LN6: N Hyk 7J 21
Raven's Vw. LN6: With S 7A 26
Ravenwood LN4: Wash 4C 18
Rayment Ho. LN6: Lin 1B 22
Raynton Cl. LN4: Wash 4C 18
Read Cl. NG24: Bald 6J 37
Reading Cl. LN4: Wash 5G 19
Rectory Cl. LN4: Pott 3A 28
Rectory La. LN4: Bran 4E 24
LN5: Wad 3E 26
Redbourne Dr. LN2: Lin 5G 11
Redcar Cl. LN6: Lin 3K 21
Redcote Dr. LN6: Lin 3K 21
Red Hall Dr. LN4: Brac B 3F 23
Red Hall La. LN4: Brac B 3F 23
Redwing Cl. LN6: Skel 3E 14
Redwing Gro. LN6: Lin 6H 15
Redwood Dr. LN5: Wad 7C 22
Reed Dr. LN2: Lin 7K 11
REEPHAM 5H 13
Reepham Rd. LN3: Fis 6J 13

Regent Av. LN6: Lin 5G 15
Regents Cl. NG23: Coll 4J 33
Regents Cres. LN1: Lin 6E 10
Regents Pk. Cl. LN6: N Hyk 6K 21
Reid Ct. LN4: Bran 2E 24
Remigius Gro. LN2: Lin 6K 11
Remus Ct. LN6: N Hyk 7G 21
Renault Dr. LN4: Brac B 5F 23
Renfrew Cl. LN5: Lin 5C 22
Renfrew Rd. LN5: Lin 5C 22
Repton Cl. LN4: Wash 5F 19
Reservoir St. LN1: Lin 1B 38 (1E 16)
Retief Cl. LN1: Lin 5D 10
Retief Vw. LN1: Lin 5D 10
Revesby Cl. LN6: Lin 1K 21
Revesby Sq. LN4: H'ton 7G 19
Reynolds Dr. LN6: Lin 1B 22
Reynolds Ho. LN6: Lin 1B 22
Richards Av. LN6: Lin 3K 21
Richmond Cl. NG24: New B 4F 37
Richmond Dr. LN6: N Hyk 4K 21
Richmond Gro. LN1: Lin 2D 16
Richmond Rd. LN1: Lin 2A 38 (2D 16)
Ridge Cl. LN2: Welt 2C 4
Ridge Vw. LN1: Lin 5D 10
 LN5: Harm .7E 26
Ridgeview Rd. LN4: Brac B 3F 23
Ridgeway LN2: Nett 2C 12
 LN4: Brac B .4G 23
Ridgewell Cl. LN6: Lin 6H 15
Ridings Cl. LN3: Fis 3K 19
Rigsmoor Cl. LN6: N Hyk 7J 21
Riley Cl. LN4: Brac B 5F 23
Ringrose Cl. NG24: N'wark T 7H 35
Ringwood Cl. LN6: Lin 5H 15
Rinks La. LN5: Bass 5B 30
Rio Dr. NG23: Coll 3H 33
Ripley Dr. LN6: N Hyk 4A 22
Ripon Cl. LN4: Brac B 3G 23
Ripon St. LN5: Lin 7C 38 (5F 17)
Risby Grn. LN6: Lin 7K 15
Rise, The LN5: Nav 5J 31
RISEHOLME .2G 11
Riseholme La. LN2: Nett, Ris 2F 11
Riseholme Rd. LN1: Lin 5F 11
Riseholme Rdbt. LN1: Lin 4E 10
Riva Bingo
 Newark-on-Trent 7D 34
Rivehall Av. LN2: Welt 1B 4
Riverdale LN2: Nett 1C 12
Rivermead LN6: Lin 3C 22
 NG24: N'wark T 2C 36
Rivermead Cl. LN6: Lin 3C 22
Riverside Dr. LN5: Lin 7A 38 (4E 16)
Riverside Lawns LN5: Lin 5D 16
Riverside Pk. NG24: N'wark T 7B 34
Riverside Rd. NG24: N'wark T 3B 36
Riverton Cl. LN1: Lin 5D 10
Riverton Vw. LN1: Lin 5D 10
River Vw. NG24: N'wark T 5E 34
Robert Dukeson Av. NG24: N'wark T 3E 34
 (not continuous)
Robertson Cl. LN5: Wad 3F 27
Robertson Rd. LN6: N Hyk 6J 21
Robert Tressell Wlk. LN2: Lin 6J 11
Robey Ct. LN5: Lin 6E 16
Robey St. LN5: Lin 6E 16
Robins Ct. NG24: N'wark T 7E 34
Robins Cres. LN6: With S 6A 26
Robinson Cl. NG24: N'wark T 7J 35
Rochester Cl. LN4: Brac B 4G 23
Rochester Dr. LN6: Lin 4H 15
Rockingham Cl. LN6: Lin 7G 15
Rolleston Cl. LN6: Lin 6F 11
Roman Cl. LN4: Meth 5J 29
 LN5: Nav 4K 31
Roman Pavement LN2: Lin 2J 17
Roman Way LN6: S Hyk 7E 20
Roman Wharf LN1: Lin 2C 16
Romney Cl. LN6: Lin 1B 22
Romney Dr. LN6: Lin 2B 22
Romulus Way LN6: N Hyk 7G 21
Rookery, The LN2: Nett 2B 12
 NG23: Coll 3H 33
Rookery Cl. LN6: With S 7A 26
Rookery La. LN6: Lin 1C 22

Rooks Cl. LN1: Sax 2D 8
Ropery, The LN1: Lin 3B 38 (2E 16)
Rope Wlk. LN6: Lin 6A 38 (4D 16)
Ropewalk LN8: Wrag 3H 7
Ropewalk, The
 NG24: N'wark T 7F 35
Rosebery Av. LN1: Lin 2D 16
Rosedale Cl. LN3: C Will 1G 19
 LN6: N Hyk .4K 21
Rosefield Cl. NG24: Bald 6K 37
Rosehill Cl. LN1: Sax 2E 8
Rose Hip Wlk. LN6: With S 7A 26
Roselea Av. LN2: Welt 2D 4
Rosemary La. LN2: Lin 4D 38 (3F 17)
Roseum Cl. LN6: Lin 2J 21
 NG24: N'wark T 5F 35
Rosewood Cl. LN6: Lin 6G 15
Ross Cl. LN2: Lin 7K 11
Rossington Cl. LN4: Meth 4H 29
Rostrop Rd. LN6: Noct 5C 28
Rothwell Rd. LN2: Lin 6F 11
Roughton Ct. LN2: Lin 5G 11
Routland Cl. LN8: Wrag 4H 7
Rowan Ct. LN4: H'ton 6F 19
Rowan Rd. LN5: Wad 6C 22
 LN6: N Hyk .4K 21
Rowans, The LN1: Sax 2D 8
 LN2: Nett 2B 12
Rowan Way LN4: Meth 4G 29
 NG24: New B 3F 37
Roxborough Cl. LN6: Lin 4J 15
Roxby Cl. LN6: Lin 1K 21
Royal Exchange Shop. Cen.
 NG24: N'wark T 7D 34
 (off Middle Ga.)
Royal Oak La. LN4: Wash 4E 18
Roydon Gro. LN6: Lin 7B 16
Ruby's Av. NG24: Bald 6J 37
Ruby's Wlk. NG24: Bald 6J 37
Ruckland Av. LN1: Lin 6E 10
Ruckland Ct. LN1: Lin 6E 10
Rudgard Av. LN3: C Will 7G 13
Rudgard Ho. LN6: Lin 3D 16
 (off The Pavilions Student Village)
Rudgard La. LN1: Lin 3A 38 (2D 16)
Rue De L'Yonne NG23: Coll 2H 33
Rufford Av. NG24: N'wark T 1D 36
Rufford Grn. LN6: Lin 6C 16
Runcorn Rd. LN6: Lin 2F 21
Runswick Cl. LN6: N Hyk 4A 22
Rupert Cres. NG24: N'wark T 1D 36
Ruskin Av. LN2: Lin 7H 11
Ruskin Grn. LN2: Lin 7H 11
Rusland Cl. LN2: Lin 4G 11
Russell Av. LN6: N Hyk 7J 21
 NG24: New B 4F 37
Russell Ct. LN1: Lin 1C 38
Russell St. LN5: Lin 1D 22
Ruston Way LN6: Lin 3D 16
Rutherglen Pk. LN1: Sax 1D 8
Rutland Av. NG24: N'wark T 2E 36
Rydal Cl. LN6: Lin 4H 15
Ryecroft LN5: Lin 5D 22
Ryland Bri. LN2: Welt 2D 4
Ryland Rd. LN2: Welt 2C 4
 LN2: Welt, Dunh 2C 4
Rylands Gdns. LN2: Welt 2D 4

S

Saddler's Cl. LN4: Meth 3H 29
Sadler Rd. LN6: Lin 1F 21
Sage Ct. LN6: Lin 6D 16
St Aiden's Rd. LN6: N Hyk 5H 21
St Albans Cl. LN4: Brac B 4G 23
St Andrew Pl. LN5: Lin 7D 38 (4F 17)
St Andrew's Cl. LN5: Lin 5F 17
St Andrews Dr. LN1: Sax 2D 8
 LN6: Lin 6C 16
St Andrew's Gdns. LN6: Lin 6C 16
St Andrew's St. LN5: Lin 7D 38 (5F 17)
St Annes Bedehouses LN2: Lin 2H 17
St Annes Cl. LN2: Lin 2H 17
St Annes Rd. LN2: Lin 2H 17
St Aubins Cres. LN4: H'ton 7G 19
St Augustine LN2: Lin 7B 12

St Augustine's Cl. NG24: N'wark T 1F 37
 (off Newton St.)
ST BARNABAS HOSPICE 1E 38 (1G 17)
St Benedicts Cl. LN6: N Hyk 5H 21
St Benedict's Sq. LN5: Lin 5B 38 (3E 16)
St Botolphs Cl. LN1: Sax 1F 9
St Botolph's Ct. LN5: Lin 6E 16
St Botolph's Cres. LN5: Lin 6D 16
St Botolphs Ga. LN1: Sax 1E 8
ST CATHERINES 7D 16
St Catherines LN5: Lin 7E 16
St Catherines Cl. NG24: N'wark T 1C 36
St Catherine's Ct. LN5: Lin 7D 16
St Catherine's Gro. LN5: Lin 7D 16
St Catherine's Rd. LN5: Lin 7D 16
St Catherine's Ter. LN6: Lin 7D 16
St Chad's Ct. LN2: Dunh 3F 5
St Claire's Ct. LN2: Lin 6G 15
St Clare's Ga. NG24: N'wark T 2E 36
St Clements Ct. LN1: Lin 1C 38
St Clement's Dr. LN3: Fis 4K 19
St Clements Pas. LN2: Lin 4E 38 (3G 17)
St Clements Rd. LN6: N Hyk 5J 21
St Crispin's Cl. LN6: N Hyk 5H 21
St Cuthberts Ct. LN2: Lin 3C 38
St David's Cl. LN3: C Will 6G 13
St Davids Rd. LN6: N Hyk 5H 21
St Edward's Dr. LN2: Scot 2H 13
St Faith's Ct. LN1: Lin 3A 38 (2D 16)
St Faith's St. LN1: Lin 3A 38 (2D 16)
St Francis's Ct. LN6: N Hyk 5H 21
St George's Cl. LN6: N Hyk 4J 21
St George's Ct. NG24: N'wark T 6E 34
St George's La. NG24: Ris 4F 11
ST GILES 7D 16
St Giles Av. LN2: Lin 1E 38 (1G 17)
St Gile's Way NG24: Bald 4J 37
St Helen's Av. LN6: Lin 7B 16
St Hilarys Cl. LN6: N Hyk 4H 21
St Hugh's Cl. LN3: C Will 6G 13
St Hugh's Dr. LN3: L'worth 5C 6
 LN6: N Hyk .5J 21
St Hugh's St. LN2: Lin 4E 38 (3G 17)
St Johns Av. LN3: C Will 6G 13
 LN6: N Hyk .5J 21
St Johns Rd. LN1: Lin 7F 11
 LN4: Brac B .4F 23
St John's Sq. LN4: Brac B 4G 23
 (not continuous)
St Leonard's Ct. NG24: N'wark T 6D 34
 (off Kirk Ga.)
St Leonard's La. LN2: Lin 2E 38 (2G 17)
St Luke's Cl. LN3: C Will 6H 13
St Margaret's Cl. LN6: Lin 3B 22
St Margaret's Gdns. LN6: Lin 3A 22
St Mark's LN5: Lin 7A 38
 LN6: Lin 6A 38 (4D 16)
St Mark's Av. LN3: C Will 6G 13
St Marks Cl. LN6: N Hyk 4J 21
St Mark's La. NG24: N'wark T 7D 34
 (not continuous)
St Mark's Pl. NG24: N'wark T 7D 34
St Marks Shop. Pk. LN5: Lin 6B 38 (4E 16)
 LN6: Lin 6A 38 (4E 16)
St Mark's Sq. LN5: Lin 6A 38 (4E 16)
St Mark St. LN5: Lin 6B 38 (4E 16)
St Martin's La. LN2: Lin 3C 38 (2F 17)
St Martin's St. LN2: Lin 3C 38 (2F 17)
St Mary's Av. LN2: Welt 1C 4
St Mary's Ct. NG24: N'wark T 7E 34
St Mary's Gdns. NG24: N'wark T 3C 36
St Marys Rd. LN6: N Hyk 5J 21
St Mary's St. LN5: Lin 6B 38 (4F 17)
St Matthews Cl. LN3: C Will 6G 13
 LN6: Lin 5D 16
St Michael Cl. LN5: Wad 3F 27
St Michaels Ter. LN1: Lin 3C 38 (2F 17)
St Nicholas St. LN1: Lin 1B 38 (1F 17)
St Paul's Av. LN3: C Will 6G 13
St Pauls Ct. LN5: Wad 3F 27
St Paul's La. LN1: Lin 2C 38 (2F 17)
St Peter at Arches LN2: Lin 4C 38
St Peters Av. LN3: C Will 6G 13
 LN6: Lin 2C 22
 LN6: N Hyk .5H 21
St Rumbold's St. LN2: Lin 5D 38 (3F 17)
St Simon's Dr. LN3: C Will 6G 13

St Stephen's Ct. LN6: N Hyk 6J 21
St Swithin's Sq. LN2: Lin 5C 38 (3F 17)
St Wilfreds Cl. NG23: N Mus 4C 32
St Wilfrid's Cl. LN4: Meth 5J 29
Salisbury Cl. LN1: Sax 2E 8
Salisbury Dr. LN4: Brac B 3G 23
Salisbury Rd. NG24: N'wark T 2D 36
Salix App. LN6: Lin 5G 15
Saltergate LN2: Lin 5C 38 (3F 17)
Salters Cl. LN4: Brac B 5G 23
Sanders Cl. LN1: Lin 5D 10
Sanders Vw. LN1: Lin 5D 10
Sandfield Way NG24: N'wark T 3B 36
Sandhills Cl. NG24: N'wark T 6C 34
Sandhills Pk. NG24: N'wark T 6C 34
Sandra Cres. LN4: Wash 5F 19
Sandringham Dr. LN8: Wrag 4G 7
Sandringham Ho. LN2: Lin 6G 11
Sands La. LN5: Carl M 6C 30
Sandtoft Cl. LN6: Lin 1H 21
Sandwell Dr. LN6: Lin 5H 15
Sanigar Ct. NG24: N'wark T 5G 35
Sansford Grn. LN6: Lin 1A 22
Sapling Cl. NG24: New B 3G 37
Saracen's Head Yd. NG24: N'wark T 7D 34
Sargent Cl. LN4: Meth 4G 29
Sastangate Ho. LN1: Lin 1B 38 (1E 16)
Satinwood Cl. LN6: Lin 5G 15
Satterley Cl. LN6: With S 7B 26
Saucemere Dr. NG24: N'wark T 2D 36
Sausthorpe Cl. LN5: Lin 5F 17
Sausthorpe St. LN5: Lin 5F 17
Saville St. LN5: Lin 7D 16
Savoy Ct. NG24: N'wark T 7D 34
Sawmill La. LN8: Wrag 3F 7
Sawyers Cl. LN8: Wrag 7F 35
SAXILBY 3E 8
Saxilby Ent. Pk. LN1: Sax 4H 9
Saxilby Rd. LN1: Bro 5E 8
   LN1: Bur, Lin ....4K 9 & 6H 9
   LN1: Lin 6A 10
   LN6: Skel 1E 14
Saxilby Station (Rail) 7F 9
Saxon Cl. LN4: Meth 5J 29
Saxon St. LN1: Lin 1B 38 (1E 16)
Saxon Vs. LN1: Lin 1E 16
Scampton Av. LN6: Lin 1K 21
Scarle Cl. LN6: Lin 5A 22
Scawby Cres. LN6: Lin 7K 15
Schoeffer Ho. LN6: Lin 6F 15
Scholars M. NG24: N'wark T 7F 35
School Cres. LN2: Scot 6G 5
School Dr. LN2: Welt 2B 4
School La. LN4: Can 6G 17
   LN4: Noct 6B 28
   LN4: Wash 4E 18
   LN5: Harm 7E 26
   LN6: N Hyk 6K 21
   LN6: T Hill 7B 20
   NG23: Thor 7A 8
Sconce Wlk. NG24: N'wark T 2C 36
Scopwick Pl. LN2: Lin 5F 11
Scorer St. LN5: Lin 5E 16
SCOTHERN 7H 5
Scothern La. LN2: Dunh 3E 4
   LN2: Scot 1G 13
   LN2: Stain L 2B 6
   LN3: L'worth 4C 6
   LN3: Stain L 2B 6
Scothern Rd. LN2: Nett ....1B 12 & 7D 4
Scott Gdns. LN2: Lin 7J 11
Scotton Dr. LN6: Lin 7A 16
Seacroft NG24: N'wark T 7J 35
Searby Rd. LN2: Lin 5H 11
Sedgebrook Cl. LN2: Lin 5F 11
Sedgebrook Ho. LN2: Lin 5F 11
Sedgemoor Cl. LN6: N Hyk 6J 21
Seely Cl. LN4: H'ton 6F 19
Selby Cl. LN6: N Hyk 4A 22
Sempers Cl. LN6: T Hill 7B 20
Seven Hills NG24: N'wark T 4E 34
Severn St. LN1: Lin 2C 16
Sewell Rd. LN2: Lin 2G 17
Sewells Wlk. LN5: Lin 5E 16
Sewstern Cl. LN4: Brac B 5G 23
Shaftesbury Av. LN6: Lin 4H 15

Shaftesbury Way NG23: Coll 3H 33
Shakespeare St. LN5: Lin 6E 16
   NG24: New B 2F 37
Shamrock Cotts. LN5: Lin 1E 22
Shannon Av. LN6: Lin 2A 22
Shannon Cl. LN6: Lin 2A 22
Shardloes LN4: Bran 3F 25
Sharp Wlk. LN6: N Hyk 7K 21
Shawbury Cl. LN6: Lin 1G 21
Shaw Way LN2: Nett 1B 12
Shays Dr. LN6: Lin 7A 16
Shearwater Cl. LN6: Lin 5J 15
Shearwater Rd. LN6: Lin 6J 15
Sheepwalk LN6: With S 4B 26
Sheepwash La. LN4: H'ton 6E 18
Sheldrake Rd. NG24: N'wark T 7H 35
Shelley Cl. NG24: Bald 5H 37
Shelley Dr. LN2: Lin 7H 11
Shelton Av. NG24: N'wark T 3C 36
Shepherds Way LN2: Scot 1H 13
Sheppard Ct. LN4: Brac B 4G 23
Sheppard's Cl. LN4: H'ton 6F 19
Sheraton Cl. LN6: Lin 7H 15
Sherbrooke St. LN2: Lin 3K 17
Sheridan Cl. LN2: Lin 6J 11
   NG24: Bald 4H 37
Sherwood Av. NG24: N'wark T 1E 36
Sherwood Dr. LN5: Wad 6D 22
Shiregate LN4: Meth 3H 29
Short Furrow LN5: Nav 5K 31
Short Wheatley La. NG23: Coll 7H 33
Shuttleworth Cl. LN6: N Hyk 7J 21
Shuttleworth Ho. LN2: Lin 3G 17
Sibcy La. NG24: N'wark T 5H 37
Sibthorpe Dr. LN2: Scot 1H 13
Sibthorpe Gdns. LN4: Can 6H 17
Sibthorp St. LN5: Lin 7B 38 (5E 16)
Side Row NG24: N'wark T 7F 35
Sidings, The LN1: Sax 3E 8
   LN6: Lin 6A 38 (4E 16)
Sidlaw Gro. LN6: Lin 5C 22
Sidney St. LN5: Lin 6E 16
Sidney Ter. LN5: Lin 6E 16
Sikorski Cl. NG24: N'wark T 6D 34
Silverstone Rd. LN6: Lin 7G 15
Silver St. LN2: Lin 4C 38 (3F 17)
   LN4: Bran 4E 24
   LN8: Wrag 3H 7
Simon's Grn. LN6: Lin 1C 22
Simon's Way LN2: Lin 3K 17
Simpson Cl. NG24: Bald 5J 37
Sincil Bank LN5: Lin 7C 38 (6E 16)
Sincil Bank Stadium 5F 17
Sincil St. LN5: Lin 6C 38 (3F 17)
Sinderson Mdws. LN6: S Hyk 7E 20
Sixfield Cl. LN6: Lin 7A 16
Skayman Flds. LN5: Carl M 7C 30
SKELLINGTHORPE 2E 14
Skellingthorpe Heritage Room 2F 15
Skellingthorpe Rd. LN1: Sax 3F 9
   LN6: Lin 4H 15
Skellingthorpe Rdbt. LN6: Lin 4G 15
Skerries Cl. LN6: N Hyk 6K 21
SKEWBRIDGE 5D 16
Skinnand La. LN5: Well 7F 31
Skipwith Cres. LN4: Meth 5J 29
Skirbeck Dr. LN1: Sax 3E 8
Slake La. NG23: S Mus 1C 34
Slaughter Ho. La. NG24: N'wark T 6D 34
Sleaford Rd. LN4: Brac B 4G 23
   LN4: Bran, Pott 4E 24
   LN4: Duns, Meth 1F 29
   LN5: Well 6H 31
   NG24: N'wark T 6E 34
Slessor St. LN5: Wad 2G 27
Smith Ho. LN4: H'ton 4D 26
Smithson Cl. NG24: New B 4G 37
Smith St. LN5: Lin 5E 16
   NG24: New B 3G 37
   NG24: N'wark T 1E 36
Smithy Yd. LN8: Wrag 3G 7
Smooting La. LN3: Ree 5J 13
Smoots, The LN5: Nav 4J 31
Smythson Grn. LN6: Dodd 5A 14
Snaith Cl. LN6: Lin 1F 21
Snaith Ct. NG24: N'wark T 6D 34
Snetterton Cl. LN6: Lin 7G 15

Snowberry Gdns. LN6: Lin 6G 15
Snowdon Cl. LN5: Lin 4D 22
Snowdon Rd. NG23: Coll 4H 33
Sobraon Hgts. LN1: Lin 6E 10
Somersby Cl. LN6: Lin 3C 22
Somerset Ho. LN2: Lin 5F 11
Somerton Ga. La. LN5: Wad 3B 26
Somerton Ri. LN5: Booth G 1J 31
Somerville Cl. LN5: Wad 1D 26
Somerville Ct. LN5: Wad 1D 26
Somme Cl. LN1: Lin 6E 10
Sorrell Ct. LN6: Lin 6G 15
Sorrel Rd. LN6: With S 7A 26
Southdown LN5: Lin 6D 22
South End NG23: Coll 5G 33
Southend Av. NG24: N'wark T 1D 36
Southfield NG24: Bald 5J 37
Southfield Ho. NG24: N'wark T 1C 36
Southfield Ter. NG24: N'wark T 1C 36
Southland Dr. LN6: Lin 3B 22
SOUTH MUSKHAM 7B 32
South Pde. LN1: Lin 3A 38 (2D 16)
   LN1: Sax 2E 8
South Pk. LN5: Lin 6E 16
South Pk. Av. LN5: Lin 6F 17
Sth. Scaffold La. NG23: Coll 7J 33
Sth. Scarle Rd. NG23: Coll 2J 33
South Vw. LN2: Dunh 3F 5
   NG24: New B 4G 37
Southwell Ct. LN4: Brac B 3H 23
Spa Bldgs. LN2: Lin 4D 38 (3F 17)
Spanby Dr. LN2: Lin 7A 16
Spa Rd. LN2: Lin 3H 17
Sparrow La. LN2: Lin 5E 38 (3G 17)
Spa St. LN2: Lin 3H 17
Speight Cl. NG24: Wint 1G 35
Spencer Cl. LN1: Sax 3G 9
Spencer St. LN5: Lin 6E 16
Spennymoor Cl. LN6: N Hyk 7H 21
Sperrin Cl. LN5: Lin 5D 22
Spilsby Cl. LN6: Lin 6H 15
Spinney, The NG24: Wint 2G 35
Spinney Cl. NG24: N'wark T 2C 36
Spinneys, The LN2: Welt 1C 4
Spirea App. LN6: Lin 6G 15
Spire Gdns. NG24: N'wark T 4F 35
Spital St. LN1: Lin 7F 11
Spring Cl. LN2: Dunh 3F 5
Spring Ct. LN2: Welt 1C 4
   LN4: Duns 2H 29
Springfield Cl. LN1: Lin 1F 17
   LN4: Bran 4E 24
Spring Gdns. NG24: N'wark T 1C 36
Spring Hill LN1: Lin 3B 38 (2E 16)
   LN3: Ree 5H 13
Spring La. NG24: Bald 4J 37
   (Gamage Cl.)
   NG24: Bald 5K 37
   (Hollowdyke La.)
Spruce Cres. LN4: Bran 3D 24
Spurr, The LN5: Well 6J 31
Squires Pl. LN5: Nett 2C 12
Squirrel Chase LN6: With S 6A 26
Stable Yd., The LN2: Nett 2B 12
Stafford Av. NG24: New B 4G 37
Staffordshire Cres. LN4: Brac B 7H 15
STAINTON BY LANGWORTH 2C 6
Stainton Gdns. LN1: Lin 6E 10
Stainton La. LN2: Scot 6K 5
   LN3: Stain L 2C 6
Stamp End LN2: Lin 5E 38 (3G 17)
Standish Ho. NG24: N'wark T 4E 36
Stane Dr. LN4: Brac B 5G 23
Stanhope Av. NG24: N'wark T 3G 35
Stanley Cres. LN4: Brac B 3F 23
Stanley Pl. LN5: Lin 5F 17
Stanley St. LN5: Lin 7D 16
   NG24: N'wark T 6F 35
Stanley Ter. NG24: N'wark T 7F 35
Stanthaket Ct. LN1: Lin 3B 38 (2F 17)
Stapleford Av. LN2: Lin 5F 11
Staple La. NG24: Bald 7F 37
Staples La. LN5: Wad 3E 26
Stark Way LN2: Lin 7K 11
Starr's Yd. NG24: N'wark T 7D 34
   (off Mill Ga.)
Station App. LN1: Sax 3E 8

Station Cl. NG23: Coll 5J 33
Station Fld. LN6: Skel 3F 15
Station Rd. LN3: L'worth 6A 6
  LN3: Ree 5H 13
  LN4: Bran 4E 24
  LN4: H'ton 7F 19
  LN4: Meth 4J 29
  LN4: Pott 7H 25
  LN5: Harm 7D 26
  LN5: Wad 1C 26
  LN6: N Hyk 4H 21
  LN6: T Hill 6A 20
  NG23: Coll 4H 33
  NG23: Harby 7D 8
Station St. LN5: Lin 6B 38 (4E 16)
Staunton Ct. LN1: Lin 3D 16
Staunton Rd. NG24: N'wark T 3D 36
Staunton St. LN1: Lin 3D 16
  (not continuous)
Staverton Cres. LN6: Lin 6F 15
Steamer Point Rd. LN4: Noct 5C 28
Steeles Dr. NG24: Bald 4J 37
Steepers, The LN2: Nett 1C 12
Steep Hill LN2: Lin 3C 38 (2F 17)
Steeping Ct. LN1: Lin 5E 10
Stenigot Cl. LN6: Lin 1G 21
Stenigot Gro. LN6: Lin 1H 21
Stenigot Rd. LN6: Lin 1G 21
Stephen Rd. NG24: N'wark T 3F 35
Stephenson Rd. LN6: N Hyk 3H 21
Stephenson Way
  NG24: N'wark T 4G 35
Stevenson Cl. LN4: H'ton 7F 19
Stewards Way LN4: Brac B 4G 23
Stewart's Yd. LN5: Lin 5C 38
Stirling Dr. NG24: Codd 5J 35
Stirling Way LN6: Skel 2D 14
Stocking Way LN2: Lin 7B 12
Stodman M. NG24: N'wark T 7D 34
Stodman St. NG24: N'wark T 7D 34
Stoke Av. NG24: N'wark T 4C 36
Stonebow Cen. LN2: Lin 4C 38
Stonecliff Pk. LN2: Welt 1B 4
Stonefield Av. LN2: Lin 1D 38 (1F 17)
Stone La. LN5: Wad 2F 27
Stonelea Cl. LN4: Bran 4F 25
Stone Moor Rd. LN6: N Hyk 7J 21
Stones La. LN6: Lin 5J 15
Stone Valley Ct. LN5: Wad 2F 27
Stoney Yd. LN5: Skel 1E 14
Stoyles Way LN4: H'ton 6F 19
Strahane Cl. LN5: Lin 4C 22
Strait, The LN2: Lin 3C 38 (2F 17)
Strawberry Hall La. NG24: N'wark T 5F 35
Strubby Cl. LN6: Lin 6H 15
Stuart Ho. LN2: Lin 6G 11
Stukeley Cl. LN2: Lin 7A 12
Stukeley Ct. NG24: N'wark T 5F 35
Sturgate Cl. LN6: Lin 7G 15
Sturton Cl. LN2: Lin 6F 11
Sturton Rd. LN1: Sax 1F 9
Sudbeck La. LN2: Welt 2C 4
SUDBROOKE 1H 13
Sudbrooke Dr. LN2: Lin 6G 11
Sudbrooke La. LN2: Nett, Scot 2C 12
Sudbrooke Rd. LN2: Scot 7G 5
Sudbury Cl. LN6: Lin 2A 22
Summers Rd. NG24: N'wark T 5E 34
Sunbeam Av. LN6: N Hyk 6H 21
Sunderland Cl. LN6: Skel 2E 14
Sunfield Cres. LN6: Lin 5H 15
Sunningdale Dr. LN6: Lin 6D 16
Sunningdale Gro. LN4: H'ton 5F 19
Sunningdale Trad. Est. LN6: Lin 5C 16
Superbowl
  Lincoln 4C 16
Sutton Av. NG24: N'wark T 4C 36
Sutton Cl. LN2: Nett 2A 12
  LN4: Wash 5C 18
Swaby Cl. LN2: Lin 5G 11
Swallow Av. LN6: Skel 3E 14
SWALLOW BECK 3K 21
Swallowbeck Av. LN6: Lin 3K 21
Swallow Dr. LN8: Wrag 4G 7
Swallow Gdns. LN6: Lin 3K 21
Swan Cl. LN2: Dunh 3E 4
Swanholme Cl. LN6: Lin 2J 21

Swanholme Lakes Local Nature Reserve
  . . . . .1J 21
Swanpool Ct. LN5: Lin 5B 38
Swanpool Garden Suburb 6A 16
Swan St. LN2: Lin 4C 38 (3F 17)
Swayne Cl. LN2: Lin 6K 11
Swaythling Cl. LN6: Lin 2J 21
Swen Cl. LN2: Welt 1D 4
Swift Gdns. LN2: Lin 6H 11
Swift Grn. LN2: Lin 6H 11
Swinburne Cl. NG24: Bald 3H 37
Swinderby Cl. NG24: N'wark T 6H 35
Swinderby Rd. NG23: Coll 4H 33
Sycamore Cl. LN3: C Will 1F 19
  LN4: Bran 2D 24
  LN6: Lin 6J 15
  NG24: Hawt 5B 36
  NG24: N'wark T 3D 36
Sycamore Cres. LN6: Lin 6J 15
Sycamore Dr. LN5: Wad 7C 22
Sycamore Gro. LN4: Brac B 5G 23
Sydney St. NG24: N'wark T 6E 34
Sydney Ter. NG24: N'wark T 1E 36
Syd Wilson Ct. LN1: Lin 6D 10
Syerston Way NG24: N'wark T 6H 35
Sykes La. LN1: Sax 1B 8
  NG24: Bald 4H 37
Sympson Cl. LN2: Lin 6A 12
Syringa Grn. LN6: Lin 5G 15
Syston Gro. LN5: Lin 3D 22
Sywell Cl. LN6: Lin 1G 21

T

Talbot Cl. LN5: Nav 4J 31
Tall Pines Rd. LN6: With S 7A 26
Tamar Way LN6: N Hyk 5A 22
Tangshan Ct. LN1: Lin 5E 10
Tanner's Ct. LN5: Lin 7A 38
Tanner's La. LN5: Lin 7B 38 (4E 16)
Tannery Wharf NG24: N'wark T 7C 34
Tapin Cl. LN1: Lin 7C 10
Tealby St. LN5: Lin 6E 16
Tedder Dr. LN5: Wad 2F 27
Teesdale Cl. LN6: Lin 4G 15
Telford Ct. NG24: N'wark T 4G 35
Telford Dr. NG24: N'wark T 4G 35
Temperance La. NG23: Coll 4G 33
Tempest St. LN2: Lin 3H 17
Temple Gdns. LN2: Lin 3D 38 (2F 17)
Ten Acre La. LN4: H'ton 2G 25
Tennyson Cl. LN4: Meth 4H 29
Tennyson Dr. LN2: Dunh 3D 4
Tennyson Ho. LN2: Dunh 3D 4
Tennyson Rd. NG24: Bald 4H 37
Tennyson St. LN1: Lin 2D 16
Tennyson Wlk. LN3: C Will 7E 12
Tentercroft St. LN5: Lin 6B 38 (4E 16)
Tentercroft St. Ind. Est.
  LN5: Lin 6C 38 (4F 17)
Tenter La. LN5: Nav 4J 31
Tenzing Wlk. NG24: Bald 4J 37
Terry Av. NG24: N'wark T 4F 35
Terry O Toole Theatre 6H 21
Tetney Cl. LN1: Lin 5E 10
Thackers La. LN4: Bran 4E 24
The . . . .
  Names prefixed with 'The' for example
  'The Alders' are indexed under the
  main name such as 'Alders, The'
Theatre Royal 4C 38
Theodore St. LN1: Lin 1A 38 (1E 16)
Theresa Ct. NG24: Bald 4H 37
Thesiger St. LN5: Lin 5F 17
Third Hill Rd. LN4: H'ton 1H 25
Thirlmere Cl. LN6: N Hyk 5A 22
Thirlmere Way LN6: Lin 4G 15
Thirsk Dr. LN6: Lin 3K 21
Thistle Cl. LN2: Lin 5J 11
Thomas Ct. LN2: Lin 3G 17
  (off Thomas St.)
Thomas Rd. NG24: Bald 6K 37
Thomas St. LN2: Lin 3G 17
Thompson Cl. NG24: Codd 5J 35
Thonock Cl. LN1: Lin 6F 11
Thonock Dr. LN1: Sax 2D 8

Thoresby Av. NG24: N'wark T 2E 36
Thoresway Dr. LN2: Lin 6G 11
Thorngate LN2: Lin 5C 38 (3F 17)
Thorngate Ho. LN2: Lin 5D 38
  (off St Swithin's Sq.)
Thornton Cl. LN4: Wash 4C 18
  LN6: Lin 7A 16
Thornton Rd. NG23: Coll 4H 33
Thorold Way LN5: Harm 7E 26
Thoroton Av. NG24: Bald 5H 37
Thoroughfare La. NG24: Wint 1H 35
Thorpe Av. LN1: Lin 6D 10
Thorpe Cl. NG24: N'wark T 4C 36
Thorpe La. LN6: S Hyk 7E 20
THORPE ON THE HILL 7B 20
Thorpe Rd. LN6: Whi 5A 20
Thorsby Cl. LN5: Wad 6D 22
Thorton Way LN3: C Will 7G 13
Thurby Rd. LN5: Bass 2D 30
Thurlby Cl. LN4: Wash 4C 18
Thurlby Cres. LN2: Lin 5H 11
Thurlow Ct. LN2: Lin 6A 12
Thyme Ct. LN6: Lin 6D 16
Tiber Rd. LN6: N Hyk 7G 21
Timms La. LN5: Wad 3E 26
Tinkermere Cl. LN2: Welt 2C 4
Tinker's La. LN5: Wad 4E 26
Tithe Barn Ct. NG24: N'wark T 6E 34
Tobruk Cl. LN1: Lin 5D 10
Tolney La. NG24: N'wark T 7B 34
Tom Otter's La. LN1: Sax 5B 8
  NG23: Harby 5B 8
Tom Ward Ct. LN1: Lin 7F 11
Top Lodge Cl. LN6: Lin 2J 21
Top Row NG24: N'wark T 7G 35
Torgate Cl. LN5: Bass 3D 30
Torgate La. LN5: Bass 3D 30
Torksey Av. LN1: Sax 2D 8
Toronto St. LN2: Lin 3J 17
Torrington Rd. LN2: Lin 5F 11
Total Fitness
  Lincoln 2F 21
Tothill Cl. LN6: Lin 7K 15
Tourist Info. Cen.
  Lincoln, Castle Hill 2C 38 (2F 17)
  Lincoln, Cornhill 5C 38 (3F 17)
Tower Av. LN2: Lin 2K 17
  LN4: Brac B 4F 23
Tower Cres. LN2: Lin 2K 17
Tower Dr. LN2: Lin 2K 17
Tower Flats LN2: Lin 2K 17
Tower Gdns. LN2: Lin 2K 17
Tower La. LN4: Brac B 7H 27
Town Hall Mus. & Art Gallery 7D 34
Townsend Way LN4: Meth 5H 29
Toynton Cl. LN6: Lin 3B 22
Trafalgar Ct. LN4: Wash 4D 18
Trelawney Cres. LN1: Lin 5E 10
Trelawney Ho. LN1: Lin 5E 10
Trenchard Sq. LN5: Wad 2G 27
Trent Cl. NG23: N Mus 4C 32
Trent La. NG23: Kel 2A 34
  NG24: N'wark T 5E 34
Trent Vw. LN1: Lin 6D 10
Trent Vs. NG24: N'wark T 2A 36
Trent Way NG24: N'wark T 5F 35
Trevose Dr. LN6: N Hyk 6K 21
Trinity Rd. NG24: N'wark T 4E 36
Trinity St. LN5: Carl M 7C 30
Tritton Retail Pk. LN6: Lin 4D 16
Tritton Rd. LN6: Lin 3K 21
Tritton Rd. Trad. Est. LN6: Lin 5C 16
Trollope St. LN5: Lin 7C 38
Troon Cl. LN4: Wash 5F 19
Troutbeck Cl. LN2: Lin 5G 11
Truro Dr. LN6: Lin 6F 15
Tryst, The NG24: N'wark T 5E 34
Tudor Cl. NG24: N'wark T 7F 35
Tudor Ho. LN2: Lin 5G 11
Tudor Rd. LN6: Lin 1H 21
Tulipwood Av. LN6: Lin 5G 15
Turnberry Cl. LN4: H'ton 6F 19
Tunbury Ct. LN6: Lin 7F 15
Turner Av. LN6: Lin 1A 22
Turner Cl. LN5: Nav 4K 31
Turner Ct. LN6: Lin 6F 15
Turner St. LN1: Lin 1A 38 (1E 16)

Turnor Cl. LN8: Wrag 3G 7
Twenty Row LN5: Nav 3K 31
Twitchell, The NG24: N'wark T 3C 36
Tyne Cl. LN6: N Hyk 5A 22

U

Uffington Av. LN6: Lin 1A 22
Uffington Cl. LN6: Lin 7A 16
Uldale Cl. LN6: Lin 4G 15
Ullswater Cl. LN6: N Hyk 5A 22
Union Rd. LN1: Lin 2B 38 (2E 16)
Unity Sq. LN2: Lin 4D 38 (3F 17)
University of Lincoln
    Brayford Campus 5A 38
    Cathedral Campus, Lindum Rd.
        . . . . .3D 38 (2F 17)
    Cathedral Campus, Wordsworth St.
        . . . . .3C 38
    Danesgate House 4C 38
    Riseholme Campus 1H 11
    Thomas Parker House 4C 38
Up. Lindum St. LN2: Lin 3E 38 (2G 17)
Up. Long Leys Rd.
    LN1: Lin 1A 38 (1E 16)
Up. Saxon St. LN1: Lin 1E 16
Urban St. LN5: Lin 1D 22
Usher Av. LN6: Lin 7B 16
Usher Gallery .3D 38
Usher Grn. LN6: Lin 1B 22

V

Valentine Rd. LN6: Lin 5C 16
Vale Vw. NG24: N'wark T 3B 36
Valiant St. LN5: Wad 3G 27
Valley Prospect
    NG24: N'wark T 2B 36
Valley Rd. LN5: Wad 7C 22
Vanwall Dr. LN5: Wad 2F 27
Vasey Cl. LN1: Sax 3G 9
Vauxhall Rd. LN4: Brac B 5F 23
Venables Way LN2: Lin 7K 11
Ventnor Ter. LN2: Lin 3C 38
Verdun Cl. LN1: Lin 6E 10
Vere St. LN1: Lin 7F 11
Vernon Av. NG24: N'wark T 7F 35
Vernon St. LN5: Lin 5D 16
    NG24: N'wark T 7F 35
Veronica Cl. LN4: Bran 3D 24
Vessey Cl. NG24: New B 4G 37
Vicarage Cl. NG23: Coll 3H 33
Vicarage Ct. LN5: Lin 5F 17
Vicarage Dr. LN6: Skel 3F 15
Vicarage La. LN2: Nett 2B 12
    LN2: Scot 7G 5
    LN2: Welt 2C 4
    LN4: Duns 2G 29
    LN5: Carl M 6C 30
    LN5: Harm 6E 26
    LN5: Well 6H 31
    NG23: N Mus 2A 32
Vicar's Ct. LN2: Lin 3D 38 (2F 17)
Victor Dr. LN6: N Hyk 6G 21
Victoria Gdns.
    NG24: N'wark T 7E 34
Victoria Gro. LN4: Wash 5F 19
Victoria Pas. LN1: Lin 3A 38 (2E 16)
Victoria Pl. LN1: Lin 3B 38 (2E 16)
Victoria St. LN1: Lin 3B 38 (2E 16)
    LN5: Lin 2D 22
    LN8: Wrag 3G 7
    NG24: N'wark T 1C 36
Victoria Ter. LN1: Lin 3A 38 (2E 16)
    NG24: N'wark T 7D 34
Victor Way LN5: Wad 3G 27
Vigo Cl. LN1: Lin 6C 10
Viking Cl. LN5: Wad 2E 26
Viking Ct. LN4: Brac B 4F 23
Viking Way LN4: Meth 5H 29
Villa Cl. LN4: Bran 4E 24
Vindex Cl. LN1: Lin 7D 10
Vine Farm Yd. NG23: Coll 3H 33
Vine St. LN2: Lin 4E 38 (3G 17)
Vine Way NG24: N'wark T 7F 35

Vixen Cl. NG24: N'wark T 4D 36
Vulcan Cres. LN6: N Hyk 5G 21
Vulcan St. LN5: Wad 2G 27

W

WADDINGTON .3F 27
Waddingworth Gro. LN2: Lin 5G 11
Wainer Cl. LN6: Lin 2G 21
Wainwright M. LN2: Lin 2E 38 (2G 17)
    (not continuous)
Wakefield Cl. LN4: Brac B 3H 23
Wake St. LN1: Lin 1E 16
Walbury Cl. LN5: Lin 5D 22
Walcot Cl. LN1: Lin 1K 21
Waldeck St. LN1: Lin 1A 38 (1E 16)
Waldo Rd. LN4: Brac B 2F 23
Walford Dr. LN6: Lin 1A 22
Walker Cl. NG24: N'wark T 1E 36
Walled Garden, The LN5: Harm 7E 26
Wallis Av. LN6: Lin 3B 22
Walmer St. LN2: Lin 3J 17
Walnut Cl. LN5: Wad 7C 22
Walnut Gth. LN3: Ree 5H 13
Walnut Pl. LN5: Lin 7C 38 (5F 17)
Waltham Cl. LN6: Lin 1G 21
    NG24: Bald 5H 37
Waltham Rd. LN6: Lin 1F 21
Walton's La. NG23: N Mus 3B 32
Warburton St. NG24: N'wark T 6E 34
Warren Ct. LN2: Lin 7K 11
Warren La. LN6: With S 6A 26
Warwick Cl. LN1: Sax 2D 8
Warwick Ct. NG24: Bald 4H 37
Warwick Rd. NG24: Bald 4H 37
Wasdale Cl. LN6: Lin 4G 15
Washdike La. LN5: Wad 7B 22
Washdyke La. LN2: Nett 2K 11
WASHINGBOROUGH 5E 18
Washingborough Rd. LN4: H'ton 6E 18
    LN4: H'ton 6G 17
Waterford La. LN3: C Will 2E 18
Waterfront, The NG24: N'wark T 1C 36
Water Hill LN3: Fis 1K 19
Water La. LN1: Lin 5B 38 (3E 16)
    LN5: Bass 2C 30
    LN6: N Hyk 7K 21
    NG24: N'wark T 6D 34
Waterloo La. LN6: Skel 4F 15
Waterloo St. LN6: Lin 5D 16
Watermill La. LN2: Nett 2B 12
Waters Edge NG24: N'wark T 5E 34
Waterside LN3: N Mus 4C 32
Waterside Nth. LN2: Lin 5C 38
    (not continuous)
Waterside Shop. Cen. LN2: Lin . . .5C 38 (3F 17)
Waterside Sth. LN5: Lin 5C 38 (3F 17)
Waterwheel La. LN4: Bran 5D 24
Watery La. LN2: Dunh 3E 4
Watling Cl. LN4: Brac B 5G 23
Wavell Rd. LN3: Lin 2K 17
Waverley Av. LN6: Lin 4K 21
Weaver Rd. LN6: Lin 2F 21
Weavers, The NG24: N'wark T 2A 36
Webb St. LN5: Lin 6D 16
Webster St. LN6: Lin 2A 22
Wedgewood Cl. LN6: Lin 7H 15
Wedgewood Gro. LN6: Lin 7H 15
Wedgewood Rd. LN6: Lin 7H 15
Wegberg Rd. LN4: Noct 5C 28
Weir Farm Paddock LN2: Scot 6H 5
Weir St. LN5: Lin 6D 16
Welbeck Av. NG24: N'wark T 6E 34
Welbeck St. LN2: Lin 3H 17
Welbourn Gdns. LN2: Lin 5G 11
Welland Cl. NG24: N'wark T 5F 35
Welland Rd. LN1: Lin 5D 10
Wellhead La. LN4: Noct 6A 28
WELLINGORE 6H 31
Wellingore Rd. LN2: Lin 5F 11
Wellington Cl. LN6: Skel 2D 14
Wellington Rd. NG24: N'wark T 7E 34
Wellington Sq. LN5: Wad 3G 27
Wellington St. LN1: Lin 2D 16
Well La. LN2: Lin 3C 38 (2F 17)
Wells, The LN2: Welt 2D 4

Wells Cl. LN4: Wash 5G 19
Wells Ct. LN1: Sax 3G 9
Wells Dr. LN4: Brac B 3H 23
Wellsykes La. LN4: Wash 7C 18
WELTON 2C 4
Welton Gdns. LN2: Lin 5F 11
Welton Rd. LN2: Nett 7A 4
Wentworth Cl. LN1: Sax 2D 8
    LN4: H'ton 5G 19
Wentworth Cnr. NG24: N'wark T 3C 36
Wentworth Ct. LN2: Dunh 4E 4
Wentworth Way LN6: Lin 7F 15
Wesleyan Ct. LN2: Lin 4D 38 (3F 17)
Wesley Cl. LN4: Meth 4H 29
    NG24: Bald 4H 37
Wesley Rd. LN3: C Will 7D 12
Westacre Ct. LN2: N Gre 5C 12
West Bank LN1: Sax 4C 8
West Bight LN1: Lin 1C 38 (1F 17)
Westbourne Gro. LN1: Lin 4A 38 (3D 16)
Westbrooke Cl. LN6: Lin 6B 16
Westbrooke Rd. LN6: Lin 6B 16
West Brook La. NG23: Coll 6G 33
Westcliffe St. LN1: Lin 7D 10
Westcroft Dr. LN1: Sax 2E 8
West Dr. LN2: Scot 1G 13
    (not continuous)
Western Av. LN1: Sax 2D 8
    LN4: Brac B 4G 23
    LN6: Lin .6B 16
Western Cres. LN6: Lin 6B 16
Western La. LN6: Skel 1D 14
Westfield App. LN2: N Gre 5C 12
Westfield Av. LN2: N Gre 5D 12
Westfield Cl. LN4: Meth 4J 29
Westfield Dr. LN2: N Gre 5C 12
West Fld. La. LN2: T Hill 7B 20
Westfield La. LN3: C Will, Ree 5E 12
    NG23: Coll 4F 33
Westfield St. LN1: Lin 3D 16
Westgate LN1: Lin 1B 38 (1E 16)
Westhall Cl. LN5: Carl M 6C 30
Westhall Rd. LN2: Welt 1C 4
Westholm LN3: C Will 1G 19
Westholm Cl. LN3: C Will 5K 11
W. Mill Ga. LN3: C Will 7G 13
Westminster Cl. LN4: Brac B 3H 23
Westminster Dr. LN4: Brac B 3H 23
Westminster Ho. LN2: Lin 5G 11
Westminster Rd. LN6: N Hyk 3H 21
West Pde. LN1: Lin 3A 38 (2D 16)
West St. LN5: Well 6H 31
West Vw. NG24: Bald 4H 37
Westway LN2: Nett 2C 12
Westwick Dr. LN6: Lin 7B 16
Westwick Gdns. LN6: Lin 1B 22
Westwood Cl. LN6: Lin 6A 16
Westwood Dr. LN6: Lin 6A 16
Wetherby Cres. LN6: Lin 3K 21
Wetsyke La. NG24: Bald 5J 37
Weymouth Cl. LN5: Lin 4D 22
Wharf, The NG24: N'wark T 6D 34
Wharf E. LN5: Lin 3E 16
Wharfedale Dr. LN6: N Hyk 4K 21
Wheatfield Rd. LN6: Lin 5G 15
Wheatley La. LN5: Carl M 7B 30
    NG23: Coll 7J 33
Wheatsheaf Av. NG24: N'wark T 3F 35
Wheel La. LN4: H'ton 7G 19
WHISBY 3A 20
Whisby Cross Roads LN6: Whi 3E 20
Whisby Natural World Cen. 6B 20
Whisby Nature Pk. 5C 20
Whisby Rd. LN6: Dodd, Whi 6A 14
    LN6: Lin, Whi 3B 20
Whisby Way LN6: Lin 2G 21
Whisby Way Bus. Cen. LN6: Lin 2G 21
Whitebeam Dr. LN6: With S 7A 26
Whitefriars Cl. LN2: Lin 7A 12
Whitefriars Rd. LN2: Lin 7A 12
Whitehall Cres. LN4: Brac B 3F 23
Whitehall Gro. LN1: Lin 3A 38 (2E 16)
Whitehall Ter. LN1: Lin 3A 38
    (not continuous)
White Hart La. NG23: Coll 4G 33
White Hart Yd. NG24: N'wark T 7D 34
    (off Market Pl.)

White La. LN5: Harm 7E 27
Whitemoor La. NG23: Coll 7C 33
Whites La. LN5: Bass 4C 30
Whitethorn Gro. LN6: Lin 5G 15
Whitfield St. NG24: N'wark T 1E 36
Whitley Cl. LN6: Skel 2E 14
Whittle Cl. NG24: N'wark T 5G 35
Whomsley Cl. NG24: N'wark T 7H 35
Wickenby Cl. LN6: N Hyk 4A 22
Wickenby Cres. LN1: Lin 6E 10
Wigford Way LN1: Lin 5B 38 (3E 16)
    LN5: Lin 5B 38 (3E 16)
Wigsley Cl. LN6: Lin 1H 21
Wigsley Rd. LN6: Lin 1H 21
Wilford Cl. NG24: N'wark T 7F 35
Wilfred Av. NG24: New B 4G 37
William Bailey Ho. NG23: Coll 4H 33
Williams La. NG24: Bald 6J 37
Williamson St. LN1: Lin 1F 17
William St. LN1: Sax 3E 8
    NG24: N'wark T 1E 36
William St. Bus. Pk. LN1: Sax 3F 9
Willingham Av. LN2: Lin 5F 11
Willis Cl. LN1: Lin 1A 38 (1E 16)
Willis Rd. NG24: N'wark T 3D 36
Willis Ter. LN1: Lin 1A 38 (1E 16)
Willoughby La. LN5: Wad 6C 22
Willow Cl. LN1: Sax 3F 9
    LN6: Skel 3F 15
Willow Cotts. NG24: N'wark T 2A 36
Willow Ct. LN4: Brac B 5G 23
    LN4: Wash 4E 18
Willow Dr. NG23: N Mus 4B 32
Willowfield Av. LN2: Nett 2C 12
Willow La. LN4: Duns 1G 29
Willow Rd. LN4: Bran 3C 24
    LN6: N Hyk 5K 21
    NG24: New B 3G 37
Willow Tree Cl. LN5: Lin 1D 22
Willowtree Gdns. LN6: Lin 6G 15
Willow Way LN2: Welt 2D 4
Wilson Ho. NG24: N'wark T 4D 36
Wilson St. LN1: Lin 1E 16
    NG24: N'wark T 6D 34
Winchester Ct. LN6: N Hyk 7H 21
Winchester Dr. LN4: Wash 5E 18
Winchilsea Av. NG24: N'wark T 1E 36
Windermere Av. LN6: N Hyk 5A 22
Windermere Rd. LN2: Lin 5J 11
Windmill Cl. LN5: Wad 4F 27
Windmill Vw. LN1: Lin 1A 38 (1E 16)
Windsor Av. NG24: N'wark T 2C 36
Windsor Cl. LN2: Scot 1H 13
    NG23: Coll 4H 33

Windsor Ho. LN2: Lin 6G 11
Win . . Pk. Cl. LN6: N Hyk 6K 21
Windsor Rd. NG24: N'wark T 1D 36
Wingrave St. LN1: Lin 7D 10
Winniffe Gdns. LN2: Lin 6K 11
Winnowsty La. LN2: Lin 2E 38 (2G 17)
Winn St. LN2: Lin 3G 17
Winstanley Dr. NG24: N'wark T 7J 35
Winster Cl. LN2: Lin 4G 11
Winston Ct. NG24: N'wark T 3C 36
Winterdale Cl. NG24: N'wark T 6H 35
Winterton Ho. LN6: Lin 7K 15
WINTHORPE 1H 35
Winthorpe Cl. LN6: Lin 7H 15
Winthorpe Gro. LN6: Lin 7H 15
Winthorpe Rd. LN6: Lin 7H 15
    NG24: N'wark T 4F 35
                                        (not continuous)
Winton Rd. LN5: Nav 5J 31
Wire Hill La. LN8: Wrag 2H 7
Wiseholme Rd. LN6: Skel 4F 15
Wisteria Av. LN4: Bran 3D 24
Witchford Cl. LN6: Lin 1F 21
Witchford Rd. LN6: Lin 1F 21
Witham Cl. LN6: Lin 2D 22
    NG24: N'wark T 5F 35
Witham Ct. LN6: Lin 5D 16
WITHAM COURT 6A 22
Witham M. LN5: Lin 7A 38 (4E 16)
Witham Pk. LN5: Lin 4H 17
Witham Pk. Ho. LN5: Lin 4G 17
WITHAM ST HUGHS 6A 26
Witham Vw. LN4: Wash 4C 18
Witham Wharf LN5: Lin 5B 38
Wittering Cl. LN6: Lin 1H 21
Woburn Av. LN1: Lin 7E 10
Wold Vw. LN2: Nett 1C 12
Wolfit Av. NG24: Bald 4J 37
Wolsey Rd. NG24: N'wark T 4E 34
Woodbank LN6: Skel 1E 14
Woodburn Cl. LN1: Lin 5E 10
Woodburn Vw. LN1: Lin 5E 10
Woodchester Ct. LN6: N Hyk 7F 21
Woodcock La. LN1: B Wat 6H 9
Woodcroft LN6: S Hyk 7E 20
Woodcroft Rd. LN1: Sax 2D 8
Woodfield Av. LN6: Lin 6F 15
Woodfield Cl. LN6: Lin 5G 15
Woodhall Cres. LN1: Sax 2D 8
Woodhall Dr. LN2: Lin 5F 11
Woodhill Rd. NG23: Coll 3H 33
Woodland Av. LN6: Skel 4F 15
Woodlands NG24: Wint 1H 35

Woodlands Cl. LN4: Pott 3A 28
    NG24: N'wark T 2C 36
Woodland Vw. LN2: Lin 2G 17
Wood La. LN6: S Hyk 6E 20
Woodpecker Cl. LN6: Skel 3E 14
Woodrush Rd. LN2: Lin 5J 11
Woods Ct. NG24: N'wark T 1E 36
Woods End LN2: Dunh 3E 4
Woodstock Cl. NG24: N'wark T 7G 35
Woodstock St. LN1: Lin 2D 16
Wood St. NG24: N'wark T 7F 35
Woodvale Av. LN6: Lin 1G 21
Woodvale Cl. LN6: Lin 1G 21
Woodwards, The NG24: New B 2G 37
Woolley Rd. LN2: Scot 1H 13
Worcester Cl. LN4: Brac B 4G 23
    LN6: Lin .7H 15
Wordsworth Dr. NG24: Bald 3H 37
Wordsworth St. LN1: Lin 3C 38 (2F 17)
Worktown Ind. Units NG24: N'wark T . . .5F 35
Worthington Rd. NG24: Bald 5J 37
WRAGBY 3G 7
Wragby Rd. LN2: Lin 3E 38 (2G 17)
    LN2: Scot 2H 13
    LN8: Wrag 1F 7
Wragby Rd. E. LN2: N Gre, Ree 6B 12
    LN3: Ree 6B 12
Wrays Yd. LN4: Noct 6B 28
Wright St. NG24: N'wark T 7F 35
Wrightsway LN2: Lin 1K 17
Wroxham Cl. LN6: N Hyk 5A 22
Wyatt Ho. LN2: Lin 7H 11
Wyatt Rd. LN5: Lin 7D 16
Wyton Cl. LN6: Lin 1F 21
Wyville Wlk. LN6: Lin 7K 15

Y

Yale Cl. LN4: Wash 5F 19
Yarborough Cres. LN1: Lin 7E 10
Yarborough Leisure Cen. 6E 10
Yarborough Rd. LN1: Lin 2A 38 (1D 16)
Yarborough Ter. LN1: Lin 1A 38 (1E 16)
Yew Tree Way NG24: Codd 5K 35
York Av. LN1: Lin 2D 16
York Cl. LN4: Wash 5F 19
York Cl. LN4: Wash 5F 19
Yorke Dr. NG24: N'wark T 5F 35
Yorke Lodge LN6: Lin 3D 16
                        (off The Pavilions Student Village)
York Way LN4: Brac B 3G 23
Youngs Av. NG24: Bald 6J 37
Youngs Cl. NG24: Codd 5J 35